T0316562

.

Media Piracy in the Cultural Economy

This book takes a Marxist approach to the study of media piracy – the production, distribution, and consumption of media texts in violation of intellectual property laws – to examine its place as an endemic feature of the cultural economy since the rise of the Internet.

The author explores media piracy not in terms of its moral or legal failings, or as the inevitable by-product of digital technologies, but as a symptom of a much larger restructuring of cultural labor in the era of the Internet: labor that is digital, entrepreneurial, informal, and even illegal, and increasingly politicized. Sketching the contours of this new political economy while engaging with theories of digital media, both critical and celebratory, Mueller reveals piracy as a submerged social history of the digital world, and potentially the key to its political reimagining.

This significant contribution to the study of piracy and digital culture will be vital reading for scholars and students of critical media studies, cultural studies, political theory, or digital humanities, and particularly those researching media piracy, digital labor, the digital economy, and Marxist theory.

Gavin Mueller was born in Columbus, Ohio. He holds a PhD in Cultural Studies from George Mason University. He currently teaches New Media and Digital Culture in the Media Studies program at the University of Amsterdam.

This is a beautifully written and engaging publication that makes a very important contribution to the growing literature on media piracy. Mueller not only examines piracy as a culturally embedded activity, but he expertly uses Marxist theory to elucidate his argument that piracy must be seem as a part of the greater reorganisation of labour in the digital era. *Media Piracy in the Cultural Economy* is essential reading for anyone interested in looking beyond purely economic concerns and instead examining how piracy is inextricably connected to wider social and political shifts.

—Virginia Crisp, King's College London

Media Piracy in the Cultural Economy

Intellectual Property and Labor
under Neoliberal Restructuring

Gavin Mueller

LONDON AND NEW YORK

First published 2019 by Routledge

2 Park Square, Milton Park, Abingdon, Oxon OX14 4RN
605 Third Avenue, New York, NY 10017

Routledge is an imprint of the Taylor & Francis Group, an informa business

First issued in paperback 2021

Publisher's note

The publisher has gone to great lengths to ensure the quality of this reprint
but points out that some imperfections in the original copies may be apparent.

British Library Cataloguing-in-Publication Data
A catalogue record for this book is available from the British Library

Library of Congress Cataloging-in-Publication Data
A catalog record has been requested for this book

ISBN: 978-1-138-30381-2 (hbk)
ISBN: 978-1-03-217823-3 (pbk)
DOI: 10.4324/9780203730720

Typeset in Times New Roman
by codeMantra

For Katie

Contents

Acknowledgments   viii

Introduction   1

1   Theories of Late Capitalist Restructuring:
    Neoliberalism and Post-Fordism   4

2   The Critique of the Digital Political Economy   28

3   A History of Digital Piracy   57

4   Theorizing Piracy   77

5   Global Piracy   99

    Conclusions: The End of P2P   114

Index   125

Acknowledgments

Any book is a collective process with contributions too numerous to name. I would like to single out several individuals, without whom this work would not have been possible. First of all, my wife and partner Katherine Casey, who bore with me through the long and difficult process of completing this work. I am also grateful for the support of my parents, Scott and Sharon, and my brother, Chad. As this book began as my dissertation project, I would like to thank Paul Smith, my dissertation chair, for pushing me on questions great and small, as well as the other members of my committee, Char Miller and J.P. Singh, for the generosity of their time and effort. I would like to extend those thanks to the other faculty and affiliates in George Mason University's Cultural Studies program, who provided a continual atmosphere of rigorous intellectual inquiry and curiosity at an enviably high level of sophistication, especially Roger Lancaster, Denise Albanese, Alison Landsberg, and Matt Karrush. Tim Kaposy and Mark Sample, who are no longer with the university, provided much appreciated early guidance. I benefited from numerous conversations and freely given insights from my peers and colleagues surrounding critical theory, economics, technology, and politics, which have left an indelible mark on this work. At the risk of leaving off names, I'd like to thank John Carl Baker, Julian Duane, Daniel Greene, Asad Haider, Geraldine Juárez, Kimberly Klinger, Larisa Mann, Wayne Marshall, Salar Mohandesi, Zac Petersen, Ryan Vu, and Björn Westergard. Finally, I'd like to thank the pirates whose projects, many now shuttered, enabled so much of this research.

Introduction

This work in this book stems from my intellectual commitments to historical materialism and to the politics embedded in popular practices. This is to say, it is both a book of Marxist theory and a work of cultural studies. I am interested in how contestatory social and cultural formations emerge from the contradictions of capitalism in our era, how they struggle, and how they shape history.

These commitments color my approach to thinking about the Internet. The categories of Marxist analysis – the commodity, property, the technologies of production, and labor – all appear in the digital realm, often in novel ways, and subject to novel theorizations, many of which I will cover in the following pages. But Marx was not simply a social theorist of capitalism. He was also a political theorist of clashes between and among classes. This informs my own theorization of the digital: it is not simply an assemblage of new technologies or new ways of doing business. It is a context for new kinds of struggles, where actors compose themselves in new ways to fight what are often much older battles.

Media piracy seemed like a social phenomenon that embodied so much of what interests me about struggles under capitalism, and it seemed so rarely understood this way. Piracy was either an activity taken by entitled miscreants, or it was an unfortunate side effect of digital technology. And Marxists had largely ignored it altogether, even while they produced much interesting analysis about digital technology. After all, Marxist politics traditionally focuses on struggles between labor and capital on the shop floor, seemingly a world away from teenagers downloading music files.

My argument is that media piracy, like much else online, can fruitfully be conceptualized in terms of labor, and that this offers us a better understanding of piracy and many other activities digital cultures engage in, and may even add depth to digital politics. In turn, a detailed understanding of struggles in online spaces helps us better understand the transformations of labor and capital, and the new politics emerging from them. In short, I want to bring the Marxists online, and I want to make the digital natives hoist a red flag.

To understand these struggles requires quite a bit of reconstruction of context, as social phenomena do not emerge autochthonously, but precipitate from prior technical, social, political, and economic relations. Therefore, I situate media piracy, and related elements of digital culture, in just such a preexisting context. My approach to laying out the proper context for digital culture is informed by historical materialism, which means I believe that, prior to what people do, say, and think with digital technology, those people must first find the means to reproduce their existence: to eat, to sleep, and to live. In our world, this means that almost everyone must work, and that work exists in an economy structured in specific ways. And so, to understand the setting from which the Internet arises, and what people learn to do with it, we must first start a bit before the rise of the personal computer, to excavate those prior relationships of work and consumption, and how they underwent dramatic transformation. I do this in Chapter 1, where I describe this transformation using the conceptual tools of neoliberalism and post-Fordism.

Chapter 2 sits like a concentric circle inside Chapter 1. This chapter reconstructs the history of intellectual property battles online grounded in the dynamics of capitalist restructuring and social struggle. Here I examine the rise of the Internet and digital media as a site of accumulation, and view the accompanying insurrections from hacker culture, the Free Software movement and the projects for copyright reform in terms of labor struggles. I do this through a critique of influential theorizations of these social struggles: the liberal reformist project of the Free Culture movement, the utopian predictions of post-Autonomist Marxism, and more recent research on digital labor, which illuminates the way that online activity is increasingly value-producing: always-already a form of work, and subject to many of the techniques of capitalist domination and exploitation.

In Chapter 3, I offer a history of digital piracy, from early computing, through Bulletin Board System (BBS) software pirates, peer-to-peer file sharing, and up to the moment of streaming media. The structure of this chapter uses the autonomist Marxist dynamic of composition-struggle-decomposition to explain the development of today's digital cultural economy. I sifted through several archives, and so this chapter will be of interest to new media historians of any theoretical or political leaning.

In Chapter 4, I critically evaluate other theories of digital piracy in an effort to discern pirate politics. Pirates have been deemed Schumpeterian disrupters, social democratic reformers, and radical accelerationists; I add my own thoughts about pirates as an example of the contemporary theory of communization.

Wary of producing a study of media piracy that limits itself to online conduct in wealthy nations, I broaden my view of piracy in Chapter 5, incorporating the forms of labor, varieties of cultural production, and kinds of struggles that happen in the Global South.

I conclude with a postmortem of sorts, where I assess the unrealized political potentials of piracy, and the wider problems in theorizations of the politics of digital culture.

1 Theories of Late Capitalist Restructuring
Neoliberalism and Post-Fordism

Work and consumption underwent massive historical changes in the decade before personal computers, changes which are necessary to understanding the politics of digital culture. Some of these changes were technological, but many were political: they had to do with massive alterations in policy and in transformations of the relations of power of different, antagonistic groups. These changes were accompanied by new ways of thinking, new kinds of values, and new frameworks for conceptualizing human behavior: in other words, new, or newly dominant, forms of ideology.

The most prevalent term for describing this momentous transformation in profit-making, work, consumption, and ideology is neoliberalism. In its etymology, "neoliberalism" refers to a revival of specific elements of classical liberal doctrine, namely the separation of the state from the economy in the form of "free markets," though a more careful historiography disputes this characterization. This chapter will situate neoliberalism within a specific historical conjuncture, that of the crisis in profits and subsequent restructuring of capitalism in the early 1970s. It will highlight the major features of neoliberalism as an ideology, one rooted in the necessities and struggles of this restructuring. That is to say, I take Karl Marx's statement in *The German Ideology*, "The ruling ideas are nothing more than the ideal expression of the dominant material relationships, the dominant material relationships grasped as ideas" seriously (192). Neoliberalism is the ideological accompaniment to economic relationships, which manifests itself as a flexible strategy of class rule.

To describe the transformations in work and accumulation, I have opted for the term "post-Fordism," as the literature on this concept engages more directly with economic structures, particularly the labor process. "Post-Fordism" was coined by the Regulation School group of economists. According to Regulation Theory, capitalist accumulation, normally riven by conflict, is stabilized according to several paradigms: an "industrial paradigm" which covers the division of labor; an "accumulation regime" entailing a pattern of production and consumption; and a "mode of regulation" encompassing institutions, organizational forms, and cultural norms which stabilize accumulation (Danielzyk and Ossenbruegge). While nominally stable, these forms may succumb to capitalism's contradictions eventually, causing restructuring of these paradigms. During the crisis of Fordism, roughly taking place in the late 1960s to early 1970s, a number of major political, legal, and economic changes were made, inaugurating the post-Fordist era of capitalist accumulation.

Before I move on to a fuller description, I want to sound a note of caution. The relation between post-Fordism and neoliberalism at first resembles the division between economic "base" and ideological "superstructure" in Marxist theory. This would mean that neoliberalism is, in some sense, simply a way to mystify the "reality" of post-Fordist economic relations, which have a greater explanatory power. However, the division of base and superstructure in Marxist theory is an untenable one. As Althusser notes,

> ...the economic dialectic is never active in the pure state; in History, these instances, the superstructures, etc. – are never seen to step respectfully aside when their work is done or, when the Time comes, as his pure phenomena, to scatter before His Majesty the Economy as he strides along the royal road of the Dialectic. From the first moment to the last, the lonely hour of the "last instance" never comes. (113)

Rather, I understand neoliberalism as a political-ideological body of thought mobilized in response to the crisis, which intersects in manifold and sometimes contradictory ways with restructuring of capitalist accumulation worldwide. In this chapter, I will analyze theories of the crisis in Fordism, and then move on to a discussion of how neoliberal philosophy inflected the transformation of Fordism at the level of state policy and subject formation.

Finally, I will examine the role of intellectual property within post-Fordist restructuring. Science, technology, and innovation are major investment concerns in post-Fordism, and intellectual property emerged as an important way for capital to both commodify and retain control over discoveries. As media and cultural production took on an expanded role in advanced economies, here too intellectual property became a means to secure revenue streams, particularly in markets in the Global South. Intellectual property is a fundamental component of neoliberal policy, though one subject to immense pressures in the form of a variety of social antagonisms to be discussed in Chapters 2 and 3.

The Crisis in Fordism-Keynesianism

While the Fordist era is typically dated from 1930 to the 1970s, Fordism takes its name from an earlier figure: Henry Ford who transformed the industrial workforce through the creation of massive factory works, assembly lines, and heavily monitored factory towns. Antonio Gramsci coined the term to describe how Ford's dominion created "a new type of man suited to the new type of work and productive process" (*Prison Notebooks* 286). At the level of production, the laboring body was tightly controlled through scientific management and mechanization. Time was organized around regular daily shifts, and a firm gendered division of labor, with women as housewives, was the rule. Rather than completely suppress unions, capital collaborated with them to stabilize production. In exchange for relinquishing control of the production process, workers would receive increasing wages to accompany increased productivity and profits.

Beyond the factory gates, consumption was also controlled. The standardization of consumer demand took the form of a "social wage," via a welfare state run according to Keynesian economic precepts to provide guarantees on employment rates, health care, public education, and pensions. Sociologist Bob Jessop characterizes Fordism as "a virtuous autocentric circle of mass production and mass consumption secured through a distinctive mode of regulation that was institutionally and practically materialised in the Keynesian Welfare National State" ("What Follows Fordism?" 292). In addition to the social wage, Fordism also relied upon "unproductive" and unwaged labor outside of formal employment. Maria Dalla Costa, in *The Power of Women and the Subversion of the Community*, argues that unpaid housework is an essential component in reproducing the workforce on a daily basis under Fordism.

In this way, capital, via the state, took an increasing role in the reproduction of the working class: on securing the means by which workers not only produced commodities, but also their health, well-being, consumption patterns, and leisure activities. Crucially, this required a strong nation state: as Jessop puts it, "congruence between national economy, national state, national citizenship, and national society; and from institutions relatively well adapted to combining the tasks of securing full employment and economic growth and managing national electoral cycles" (*Knowledge, Space, Economy* 67).

However, by the late 1960s, Fordism – which, as Alain Lipietz notes, was always a contingent and unstable relationship – went into crisis, which deepened into the next decade. "Stagflation," the simultaneous rise in inflation and unemployment, was coupled with an inexorable fall in the profits returning to capital. The period of "a long wave with an undertone of expansion" described by economist Ernest Mandel was coming to close (472). Technological progress slowed and worker productivity fell, leading to a slowdown in profit accumulation. By the 1970s, global capitalism's profit rate was in steep decline. By Fred Moseley's estimate, the rate of profit had declined 50% between 1950 and 1970 (161).

In Volume 3 of *Capital*, Marx discusses the tendency of the rate of profit to fall as an inherent quality of capitalist economies, a phenomenon recognized by classical economists such as David Ricardo. Capitalists introduce constant capital, in the form of technology and machines, into the production process, thus reducing the need to deploy variable capital: in other words, living labor in the form of waged workers. The proportion of constant capital to variable capital rises.

> Since the mass of the employed living labour is continually on the decline as compared to the mass of materialised labour set in motion by it, i.e., to the productively consumed means of production, it follows that the portion of living labour, unpaid and congealed in surplus-value, must also be continually on the decrease compared to the amount of value represented by the invested total capital. Since the ratio of the mass of surplus-value to the value of the invested total capital forms the rate of profit, this rate must constantly fall. (211)

The rate of profit in capitalism can be represented by the equation $P = s/(v + c)$, where s is the surplus value, v is the variable capital, and c is the constant capital. Marx subsequently reconfigures this equation by dividing the numerator and denominator by v, rendering it $(s/v)/(c/v + 1)$. If constant capital rises while surplus value remains the same, the rate of profit will decline. Yet as Michael Heinrich notes, Marx's theory itself is incomplete. There is no way to determine definitively that surplus value (s) always declines at a faster rate than potential declines in the value of labor power combined with constant capital (c + v) ("Crisis Theory, the Law of the Tendency of the Profit Rate to Fall, and Marx's Studies in the 1870s"). This uncertainty is reflected in Marx's contradictory name for the phenomenon: the *law* of the *tendency*.

Marxist commentators have offered a number of explanations and analyses of the crisis in Fordism. Gerard Duménil and Dominique Lévy argue that capitalists had overinvested in constant capital: "Although mechanization made labor productivity growth possible, its cost limited its potential in terms of profitability. Mechanization may have turned out to be effective in making it possible to save labor but it was expensive" (33). Robert Brenner points out that by the 1960s, Europe and Japan had finally rebuilt the industrial capacity that had been destroyed in World War II, leading to pressures of international competition. Jessop ties this to the "internationalization of trade, investment, and finance" during the globalization of capitalist production, leading to a crisis of the Keynesian state, which depended on national economies and currencies. The result was that "the wage (both individual and social) came increasingly to be seen as an international cost of production rather than as a source of domestic demand" (68). George Caffentzis points out that the loss of relevance of wages for capitalist regulation is a result of the transition to export-oriented economies: "When export of commodities becomes a central objective of capitalists, they become less concerned with the capacity of their workers to consume their products" (37).

Many of these explanations, Marx's included, focus on endogenous tendencies within capitalism. However, a renegade tendency of Marxist analysis emerging from the *operaismo* ("workerism") movement in Italy offers an addendum, if not an outright alternative, to these diagnoses. Sometimes referred to as "autonomist Marxism" in the English-speaking world, these theorists did not believe that capitalism is its own gravedigger. Rather, it must be buried. In this sense, the struggle of workers against exploitation contributed to the crisis of Fordism-Keynesianism: what Mandel describes as "class struggle attack[ing] the rate of profit" (132). For autonomist Marxist theory, all crises in capitalism result from class struggle. Mario Tronti would put it this way, inverting the trajectory of traditional Marxist theory:

> We too have worked with a concept that puts capitalist development first, and workers second. This is a mistake. And now we have to turn the problem on its head, reverse the polarity, and start again from the beginning: and the beginning is the class struggle of the working class. At the level of socially developed capital, capitalist development becomes subordinated to working class struggles; it follows behind them, and they set the pace to which the political mechanisms of capital's own reproduction must be tuned. ("Lenin in England")

In Tronti's "Copernican revolution," it is workers themselves, in their myriad rebellions, who precipitate crises in capitalism, spurring capital to develop methods to route around these rebellions. And the end of Fordism saw no shortage of rebellions. Strikes reached a peak in 1974 (Moseley 162), the same year that anti-colonial movements in Africa managed to reverberate back to the capitalist core, causing the fall of Portugal's government. The decolonization of the Global South sapped the capitalist core of reliable markets and cheap natural resources, not the least of which was oil, as the 1973 embargo rammed home.

Importantly, at this conjuncture, new vectors of struggle appeared in the industrialized world in the form of "new social movements," from the mobilizations of unwaged housewives, to the rebellions in African-American ghettos, to students organizing against the war, and to the antinuclear movement. These struggles often targeted social institutions such as the family, the university, and the military, rather than the workplace, and so the relevance of these struggles was not always understood by socialist and communist movement theory, which tended to prioritize the struggles of a specific type of worker: the one located at the immediate point of production (often in the figure of the "blue-collar" factory worker).

Tronti and other Marxist theorists of the Italian extraparliamentary left developed an analysis of the importance of processes of production and social reproduction beyond the workplace into a concept: the social factory (Gill and Pratt). According to this analysis, capitalism relies not merely on productive labor at the point of production, but also the myriad practices which reproduce capitalism and which, under Fordism's Keynesian demand management, were subject to increasing intervention from the state and from business. Nick Dyer-Witheford summarizes the autonomist position: "Tronti, writing in the 1960s, argued that capital's growing resort to state intervention and technocratic control had created a situation where 'the entire society now functions as a moment of production'" (134). Capitalism and the state had extended control beyond the workplace to the routines, capacities, and organization of the population outside it, the points of struggle for new social movements.

Harry Cleaver explains the social factory thesis as "productive consumption":

> Capital tries to shape all "leisure," or free-time, activities – language, literature, art, music, television, news media, movies, theatres, museums, sports – in its own interests. Thus, rather than

viewing unwaged "non-labour time" automatically as free time or as time completely antithetical to capital, we are forced to recognize that capital has tried to integrate this time, too, within its process of accumulation so that recreation is only the re-creation of labour-power. Put another way, capital has tried to convert "individual consumption" into "productive consumption" by creating the social factory. (123)

Cleaver's critique of leisure echoes other theorists such as Theodor Adorno and Guy Debord, who also recognized "free time" as an extension of capitalist social relations. Marx too implies this in the *Grundrisse*, describing production and consumption as two essential moments of the capitalist process: "Production is thus at the same time consumption, and consumption is at the same time production.... consumption in its turn furthers production by providing for its products the individual for whom they are products" (278). As Stuart Hall interprets Marx, "Production, then, forms objectively the modes of appropriation of the consumer, just as consumption reproduces production as a subjectively experienced impulse, drive or motive" (123). In other words, consumptive practices have a hold over production, making consumption an important site of struggle.

The social factory thesis allows diverse struggles, even those not involved at the direct process of production, to be understood as part of the larger struggle between the working classes and capital, part of the crisis in Fordism-Keynesianism. As Dyer-Witheford puts it, "Understood in the light of autonomist analysis, these diverse eruptions, while distinct, are not disconnected. Rather, they appear as a broad revolt by different sectors of labour against their allotted place in the social factory" (148).

This perspective represents a radical reformulation of the notion of class opposed to Marxist political organizations. Instead of identifying the working class as "productive" labor (or even more specifically, as the "blue-collar" industrial proletariat), autonomists analyzed the ways struggles themselves worked to constitute the category of "working class": the class that seeks to abolish the present state of things. As the first issue of the autonomist journal *Zerowork* put it, "for us, as Marx long ago, the working class is defined by its struggle against capital and not by its productive function" (3). Struggle itself was located, not in the political initiatives of worker organizations such as trade unions and labor parties, but in what Tronti dubbed the strategy of refusal: a refusal to work, a refusal to submit to capitalist social relations.

In the autonomist account, class was not a pre-established category (either ontologically, or one produced at the point of capitalist production), but was rather a continual emergence of organized struggle, according to the class's technical composition (the way the working classes are inserted into a technologically determined labor process) and its political composition (the actual concrete forms of struggle). Capital then responds to this struggle by decomposing the class. This can be done via direct repression, such as imprisonment or violence. It can also be accomplished by restructuring the labor process to reduce the ability of workers to rebel by altering how they produce and reproduce themselves. Capital accomplishes this by introducing new technologies to the labor process, which can fragment worker organizations, disempower workers by deskilling them, and reduce their numbers by automating tasks. As Cleaver describes it,

> Class composition is in constant change. If workers resisting capital *compose* themselves as a collectivity, capital must strive to *decompose* or break up this threatening cohesion. It does this by constant revolutionising of the means of production – by recurrent *restructurings*, involving organisational changes and technological innovation that divide, deskill or eliminate dangerous groups of workers. But since capital is a system that depends on its power to organise labour through the wage, it cannot entirely destroy its antagonist. Each capitalist restructuring must recruit new and different types of labour, and thus yield the possibility of working class recomposition involving different strata of workers with fresh capacities of resistance and counter-initiative. (133)

For the autonomists writing at the time, decomposition meant that the "mass worker" of Fordism described by Gramsci was rapidly becoming a relic of the past. A new worker subjectivity was being produced in its place. Antonio Negri termed this "the social worker," referring to the extreme socialization of labor as a result of technology and state intervention in the reproduction of the working class. All manner of activities could be understood as subject to capitalist exploitation, and all manner of struggles could be conceived of as class struggles ("Archaeology and Project: The Mass Worker and the Social Worker" 48). Other autonomists had similar, but distinct, diagnoses. Sergio Bologna noted that class struggles often played out at the level of urban communities (echoed by Cherki and Wieviorka, who saw collaboration between unions and neighborhoods in struggles over social services). Bologna, more cautiously than Negri, noted a "chain of infinite decentralization," as factories themselves were decomposed into smaller units, driving many workers into universities or marginal sectors (54).

French sociologists Eve Chiapello and Luc Boltanski, while not part of autonomism, have developed an account of post-Fordism consonant with Tronti's precept that the motor of capitalist development runs on the struggle and demands of workers. They identify two strands of critique developed in the crisis of Fordism (specifically the Paris uprising of May 1968). Protesters in Western nations deployed an "aesthetic critique of capitalism" prioritizing creative self-expression and spontaneity against the anomie and degradation of Taylorized bureaucratic firms, as well as a "social critique of capitalism," focusing on exploitation and discrimination.

According to Chiapello and Boltanski's account, capitalism had a much easier time responding to the aesthetic critique, with its emphasis on dehumanizing instrumental rationality, than the social critique, which went to the heart of capitalism's need to expropriate surplus value from workers. Features of post-Fordist management philosophy such as "leanness" and quality control circles, which allow workers to voice their opinion on their work, emerge from grappling with the aesthetic critique of capitalism, with its desires for creativity and participation. The ideal post-Fordist arrangement became "lean firms working as networks with a multitude of participants, organizing work in the form of teams or projects, intent on customer satisfaction, and a general mobilization of workers thanks to their leaders' vision" (73). Workers "must be organized in small, multi-tasked teams" which are "more skilled, more flexible, more inventive and more autonomous than" the more rigid hierarchies of Fordism (74).

In this way, capital met the desires by workers and students to have more creative, meaningful working lives by decomposing the mass working class, and restructuring accumulation to satisfy the aesthetic critique, rather than deal with the demands of the social critique. As Albert Toscano put it, "the flight from the factory is turned into an opportunity for profitable technological leaps and the exploitation of a de-unionized 'flexible' work force." However, the facts of post-Fordist restructuring do not always bear out the observations of management philosophy. Before I further discuss the recomposition of the working class, I will sketch the contours of economic restructuring in the post-Fordist period.

Restructuring Capitalism: Innovation and Experimentation

If Marx's account of the tendency of the rate of profit to fall is incomplete, he provides a clearer guide to the restructuring process. In the chapter, after his discussion of the tendency of the rate of profit to fall, Marx identifies "counteracting influences" to this tendency: methods to which capitalism resorts in its efforts to restore the profit rate. Technology can intensify exploitation by raising productivity enough, though this also has the tendency to wear out machines faster. Machinery can become cheaper. Commodities themselves can become cheaper, reducing the labor time necessary to reproduce the workforce. An increase in the supply of labor could depress wages; new avenues of commodification could be explored ("new lines of production are opened up, especially for the production of luxuries," 277), and finally, commodities can be exported to less productive zones, thus realizing a profit.

Understood through the autonomist rubric of composition and decomposition, Marx's counteracting influences on the falling rate of profit work to decompose existing bases of worker intransigence and route around the struggle. During the crisis in Fordism, capital's counteroffensive took place on a variety of fronts: the workplace, the state, the home, and ideology were all restructured in the face of historic militancy.

One way this restructuring has been discussed in both supportive and critical literature is the word "innovation." Innovation was initially identified by political economist Joseph Schumpeter as a major driver behind capitalism's dynamic productivity, and a number of commentators have pointed to Schumpeter's influence in contemporary business and economics. As Bob Jessop argues, the post-Fordist state's "orientation can be described as Schumpeterian because it promotes innovation, competitiveness, and entrepreneurship tied to long waves of growth and to the more recent pressures for perpetual innovation" (*Knowledge, Space, Economy* 74). Tony Smith points to the Schumpeterian imperative which "institutionalizes a continuous search for innovations that lower the costs of constant capital" (29). Innovations such as lean production, just-in-time production, subcontracting, and outsourcing are all means by which businesses reduce waste and excess stock. Innovations in communication technology facilitate offshoring of production by maintaining global systems of coordination. A continuous automation process accelerates turnover time and drives down wages by reducing the workforce. These innovations are all counteracting influences as Marx described them.

Yet the form these innovations take varies widely, and analysts have struggled to describe a distinct post-Fordist paradigm. A number of potential candidates, from "disorganized capitalism" (Lash and Urry), the "knowledge economy" (Drucker), or the "information economy" (Castells), are limited in their ability to identify patterns across the entire landscape of global capitalist production. Even specific industries, such as automobile manufacture, resist simple categorization. Instead, capitalism's restructuring appears uneven and contingent.[1] John Tomaney, in his survey of the literature, maintains that evidence is insufficient to draw out overarching trends, and that changes in work structure are "more incremental and evolutionary than is implied by concepts such as 'post-Fordism'" (176). In fact, better than "evolutionary," with an implied teleology, a better term might be experimental. As Jamie Peck and Adam Tickell argue, post-Fordism is a "search" for new fixes: "a demonstrably reproducible replacement has yet to stabilize," and capitalism continues to experiment, while lurching from crisis to crisis (280).

Some large trends in restructuring stand out. Analysts agree that capitalist firms have abandoned vertical integration, disaggregating productive activities among globally dispersed subcontracted units. Some commentators have mistaken this flexibility for disorganization (Lash and Urry) or decentralization (Hardt and Negri). However, in spite of relinquishing direct control over production, the disaggregating effects have preserved, and even deepened control. As Bennett Harrison states,

> in many cases the legally independent small firms from which the big companies purchase parts, components, and services may not be all that independent, after all, but should rather be treated as de facto branch plants belonging to big firms. Production may be decentralized into a wider and more geographically far-flung number of work sites, but power, finance, and control remain concentrated in the hands of managers of the largest companies in the global economy. (47)

Kim Moody describes this as "Greater hierarchical business control, but more flexible specialization underneath" (75). It is this flexibility, in my view, which makes generalizing a post-Fordist regime of accumulation so challenging if not impossible: there are numerous new (and old) forms of productive processes in a variety of sectors. As David Harvey puts it in *The Condition of Post-Modernity*,

> Organized subcontracting, for example, opens up opportunities for small business formation, and in some instances permits older systems of domestic, artisanal, familial (patriarchal), and paternalistic ("god-father", "guv'nor" or even mafia-like) labour systems to revive and flourish as centerpieces rather than as appendages of the production system. (152)

Subcontracting allows for hybrid articulations of productive arrangements, making it difficult to generalize a distinctly post-Fordist mode of production. This experimental nature of post-Fordism makes Harvey's formulation of "flexible accumulation" a preferable heuristic, as it captures the flux of post-Fordist production:

> Flexible accumulation, as I shall tentatively call it, is marked by a direct confrontation with the rigidities of Fordism. It rests on flexibility with respect to labour processes, labour markets, products, and patterns of consumption. It is characterized by the emergence of entirely new sectors of production, new ways of providing financial services, new markets, and, above all, greatly intensified rates of commercial, technological, and organizational innovation. It has entrained rapid shifts in the patterning of uneven development, both between sectors and between geographical regions, giving rise, for example, to a vast surge in so-called "service sector" employment as well as to entirely new industrial ensembles in hitherto underdeveloped regions. (147)

Such flexibility allows capital to flow into the most profitable sectors as quickly as possible, without ties to specific product lines, labor markets, national economies, or geographies. But establishing this "absolute reign of flexibility" as Pierre Bourdieu dubs it ("The Essence of Neoliberalism"), requiring a concerted political effort to alter the relationship between state and economy dictated by Keynesian economic philosophy. This political-ideological project is known as neoliberalism.

Neoliberalism

Neoliberal doctrine originates in the Mont Pélerin Society, an anti-socialist intellectual group which included Friedrich Hayek, Milton Friedman, and Ludwig von Mises. Founded in 1947, at the peak of Keynesianism's influence over economic policy, the society busied itself training and placing its ideologues in think tanks and state agencies awaiting an opportune moment to bring their free market philosophies to fruition. In the 1950s, they had referred to themselves as "neoliberals," but by the time the crisis of the 1970s set in, they had made the claim that their ideas could be traced to the classical liberalism of Adam Smith (Mirowski, *Never Let a Serious Crisis Go to Waste* 29). They advocated for a bundle of policy changes, largely centered around the implementation of markets and the restraining of state regulation of the business.

A long, complex body of thought without internal consistency, neoliberalism, like post-Fordism, has proven difficult to pin down. Marxist critics often point toward the forcible implementation of market competition throughout the economy, a way of undoing Keynesian demand management, what David Harvey calls "deregulation, privatization, and withdrawal of the state from many areas of social provision" (*A Brief History of Neoliberalism* 3). Harvey likens this to a return to neoclassical economics. However, Philip Mirowski, chronicler of the neoliberal "thought collective," argues that this both misrepresents neoliberal economics and commits "[t]he fallacy of identifying neoliberalism exclusively with economic theory" ("Postface: Defining Neoliberalism" 427).

In spite of its emphasis on government deregulation, neoliberal doctrine in no way opposes the state in favor of neoclassical laissez-faire economies. Milton Friedman made this clear in 1951:

> A new ideology... must give high priority to real and efficient limitation of the state's ability to, in detail, intervene in the activities of the individual. At the same time, it is absolutely clear that there are positive functions allotted the state. The doctrine that, on and off, has been called neoliberalism and that has developed, more or less simultaneously in many parts of the world... it is precisely such a doctrine... But instead of the 19th century understanding that laissez-faire is the means to achieve this goal, neoliberalism proposes that competition will lead the way. (Quoted in Mirowski, *Never Let a Serious Crisis Go to Waste* 38)

Rather than a project of undoing regulation and unfettering markets, neoliberalism is, in the words of Wendy Brown, "a constructivist project: it does not presume the ontological givenness of a thoroughgoing economic rationality for all domains of society, but rather takes as its task the development, dissemination, and institutionalization of such a rationality" (9). In this, it diverges from classical liberalism, such as that of Adam Smith, who believed in humanity's "natural propensity to truck, barter, and trade." Jessop sounds a similar note: neoliberalism "involves enhanced state intervention to roll forward new forms of governance that are purportedly more suited to a market-driven economy" ("Liberalism, Neoliberalism, and Urban Governance" 454). Neoliberal praxis, in Brown's words, focuses on "extending and disseminating market values to all institutions and social action" rather than simply the economy per se (7).

Brown draws from Michel Foucault's analysis of neoliberalism as governmentality, which he delineated in his 1978–1979 lectures at the Collége de France, collected into the volume *The Birth of Biopolitics*. Foucault offers a compelling reading of a number of important neoliberal intellectuals, including economist and Mont Pélerin Society member Gary Becker, who, he argues, was not merely crafting an economic doctrine, but creating a new theory of the human subject. Foucault analyzes this "subject of interest," the *homo oeconomicus* constructed by Becker's work, who, as an "entrepreneur of himself [sic]" treats every action as a potential to accrue "human capital": attributes "that in one way or another can be a source of future income" (224). This entrepreneurial subject pragmatically "accepts reality" in the form of "respond[ing] systematically to modifications in the variables of the environment" (269). The irony at the heart of homo oeconomicus is that while the subject "must be left alone" to make choices, the subject's rational interest "converges spontaneously with the interest of others" who are also rational (270). Thus, "homo oeconomicus is eminently governable" via "a governmentality which will act on the environment and systematically modify its variables" (270, 271), and thereby altering the predictable reactions of the rational individual.

Loïc Wacquant criticizes the governmentality approach for the vagueness of formulations such as Ong's "governing through calculation" (4), as well as the locating of neoliberal techniques in non-state institutions. Instead, he argues that neoliberalism can be understood less as consensual than as coercive, an "articulation of state, market, and citizenship that harnesses the first to impose the stamp of the second on to the third" (71): state power impresses market directives on to the individual via a series of ideological interpellations, gateways to necessary resources, and direct coercion. This is, to a great extent, a pushback against theories of neoliberalism that emphasize the reduction in state regulation. Instead, according to Wacquant, the state increases regulation over individuals (particularly at the lower ends of the socioeconomic spectrum), while doing away with Keynesian restrictions on business and trade.

Part of this state project is what Wacquant dubs the "disciplinary social policy" of "corrective workfare, under which social assistance is made conditional upon submission to flexible employment" (72). This means undergoing evaluations, training, low-paid and unpaid works, and following "behavioral mandates" such as family planning and obeying the law. In this way, all activities under neoliberalism take on the veneer of work: the individual must constantly manage risk and responsibility in rational ways to maximize outcomes and enhance human capital. The social factory described by the autonomists falls under an insidious new form of management: one's own self.

While Wacquant correctly critiques the vagueness of some governmentality formations, and emphasizes the power of the state, he lacks a strong description of the neoliberal subject. While he notes that "individual responsibility" becomes a "motivating discourse and cultural glue" (72), he doesn't connect this to subjectivity, what Brown calls "the moral subject as an entrepreneurial subject" (19). This, I shall argue, is an essential key to understanding the way in which the workforce has been recomposed by capital since the end of Fordism-Keynesianism. But subject formation does not occur merely at the level of ideology. It is embedded in specific productive arrangements. Post-Fordism and neoliberalism connect at the level of the informal.

Informal Economies and the Entrepreneurial Restructuring of the Working Class

Capital attempted to decompose the workforce by breaking up Fordism-Keynesianism: it transformed mass production, and its unruly mass worker, into more dispersed productive chains while drawing upon an eclectic mix of organizational techniques. As production dispersed and globalized, management of workers depended less exclusively on mass-production-based strategies such as scientific management; instead, it relied on other forms of domination and control through divisions of gender, kinship, and ethnicity. Harvey refers to production rooted in families or communities as "ancient forms of labor process" which "undermine working-class organization and transform the objective basis for class struggle" by fragmenting the working class (153). Yet this presumes that capital structures the wage relationship according to contractual "free labor," with other forms appearing as chronological atavisms. In fact, capitalism has always made use of "older" forms of oppression and division in structuring its labor force. For instance, the Subaltern Studies group has extensively documented the ways in which colonial industrial production drew upon not only previously existing religious, caste, and gender cleavages, but also the ways in which "this structure of relations was systematically reproduced under conditions of colonial capitalism" (Chatterjee 72), what Immanuel Wallerstein has referred to as the pervasiveness of "semi-proletarian households" even in contemporary capitalism (27).

This transformation of production into dispersed units organized according to familial, community, and ethnic ties is part of a more general sociological phenomenon: the rise of informal economies. As Castells and Portes define it, the informal economy is "a specific form of relationships of production" which "is unregulated by the institutions of society, in a legal and social environment in which similar activities are regulated" (12). The lack of regulation could manifest itself in the status of labor (undeclared, without benefits, low pay), the conditions of work (hazardous, located in areas zoned for other uses), or the form of management (off the books, patriarchal) (13). Research on the informal economy from a variety of contexts and perspectives concludes that rather than an atavism, informal economies represent a persistent structural feature in contemporary capitalist economies, including advanced ones. Furthermore, the formal and informal are articulated together. To take one example, Saskia Sassen documents how informal relations pervade construction, electronics manufacture, furniture, and the garment industry; they also extend to services such as auto repair and taxis. Sassen argues that informality often characterizes labor relations in immigrant communities, which develop into "neighborhood subeconomies" and sources of low-cost labor (71, 73).

This illuminates another facet of the social factory thesis: with informal economies, production extends beyond the factory walls into the spatiality of everyday life. Operating in the interstices where increasingly hamstrung state regulators and union officials can't find them, working from homes, garages, sweatshops, and often undocumented, workers in the informal economy stand in stark contrast to the Fordist mass worker, a *ne plus ultra* of restructuring of the working class since the crisis in Fordism. The heterogeneity of the informal economy, particularly in its articulation of labor relations with family status, ethnicity, and gender, means that "class structure becomes blurred" (Castells and Portes 31).

Is it possible to describe the deformalization of working arrangements, instead of the absence of the old, as the birth of something new? In other words, if the Fordist "mass worker" is no more, what figure arises in its place? The proliferation of subcontracting under post-Fordism, the ways in which subcontracting occurs at an informal rather than formal level, and the pressure workers face to constantly acquire new employment perfectly align with the neoliberal emphasis on the entrepreneurial self. Interpellating workers as entrepreneurs vending their human capital is not merely an ideological trick, but a method of adapting subjects to a material environment saturated with entrepreneurship: an entrepreneur, by assuming risk, has no guarantees of success, let alone stability.

The ideal post-Fordist-neoliberal society will be one made up of entrepreneurs, not workers. Bereft of regulation by government or organized labor, these entrepreneurs can respond flexibly to the demands of larger capitals and corporations, and can reduce expenditures (via low wages and tax avoidance) while opening up new markets and new commodities. Indeed, a literature extolling the entrepreneurial acumen rife in the informal economy has sprung up. Following Hernando de Soto's influential *The Other Path*, books like Robert Neuwirth's *The Stealth of Nations* marvel at the ingenuity of the entrepreneurs of "System D." Rather than view informality as a "shadow" of the main economy, it is entirely possible that informality could become the hegemonic form of labor relations in the future.

Intellectual Property and the Crisis

Intellectual property has existed in capitalist economies from their outset, but it takes on a new expanded role in the context of post-Fordism and neoliberalism as a potential source of profits in the context of a faltering profit rate. As many commentators point out, intellectual property serves to commodify knowledge, aligning scientific production further with the market-based prerogatives of neoliberalism. John Frow points to how information, rather than made accessible via public institutions such as libraries, "is increasingly managed within a system of private ownership where access is regulated by the payment of rent" (89). Scientific discoveries such as pharmaceuticals, medical technology, and even genetic material have been rendered, via patents, into private property: what Frow calls "an industrial conception of living matter which subordinates it to the commodity form" (93).

The post-Fordist emphasis on innovation presents a contradiction for capitalism. As Marx notes in *Theories of Surplus Value*, the costs to produce innovation dramatically outweigh the costs for reproducing that knowledge: "The product of mental labour – science – always stands far below its value, because the labour-time needed to reproduce it has no relation at all to the labour-time required for its original production. For example, a schoolboy can learn the binomial theorem in an hour" (353). This is a problem because the innovator can only secure surplus profits as long as they retain exclusive control over that innovation. Copyright and patents help to prevent innovations from spreading to potential competitors.

This is particularly crucial in the context of the post-Fordist disaggregation and globalization of production, where intellectual property has become a point of conflict. As manufacturing heads overseas, firms must maintain a tighter grip on their trademarks, patents, and copyrights, which keep profits flowing back to the Global North, even as many jobs go abroad. Intellectual property now counts as a chief component of US economic dominance, by separating manual from intellectual labor and guarding the products of intellectual labor with strong property rights. In other words, the Schumpeterian imperatives adopted by post-Fordist firms mean innovation is now a chief source of value and wealth, and such scientific discoveries must be jealously held to secure competitive advantage.

Media and cultural production are an excellent example of how intellectual property rights go beyond simple commodification and affect the organization of global labor and consumption. A prior theory of "cultural imperialism" presumed that US tastes in Disney and Coca-Cola could be imposed upon passive populations. A critical understanding of intellectual property and cultural production reveals how governance mechanisms privilege Northern cultural production through the organization of production and consumption. Global treaties such as the Agreement on Trade-Related Aspects of Intellectual Property Rights (TRIPS) and multinational institutions like the World Bank and the World Trade Organization facilitate relations of production beneficial to Northern firms, as David Hesmondhalgh describes:

> The spread of copyright, along the lines defined in TRIPS and in the visions of advocates of stronger copyright, both within advanced industrial countries and in other societies, means that in more and more places the prevailing conceptions of what constitutes creative or cultural work begin to shift towards the individual property model, and away from a notion of social or collective creativity. ("Neoliberalism, Imperialism, and the Media" 104)

Economically, the imposition of Western, particularly US, culture reveals the same kind of unequal exchange that characterizes imperialism. According to Miller et al., the US effectively subsidizes its own film industry via tax credits, "then seeks to destroy foreign competition by arguing that it should follow laissez-faire rules" (96). In this sense, global intellectual property rights are another instance of what Mirowski describes as the "double truth" of neoliberalism: "that a society dedicated to liberal ideas had to resort to illiberal procedures and practices" and "that a society that held spontaneous order as the ne plus ultra of human civilization had to submit to heavy regimentation and control" (68–70). And in addition to erecting favorable norms and definitions of cultural production, these agreements instantiate an unequal division of labor between North and South, what Miller et al. call a New International Division of Cultural Labor (NICL), where low-cost works, such as postproduction, occur in the South, while value is shifted to forms of employment, such as marketing and branding, located in the North.

Yet cultural work itself is degraded in the neoliberal conjuncture. Indeed, if post-Fordism lacks an identifiable ideal type in industrial manufacture, analysts of cultural labor are quite clear: cultural work exemplifies the post-Fordist tendencies of a lean self-disciplining labor force supplemented by informal and temporary workers, disaggregated production, destruction of organized labor, and the imposition of labor-replacing technology. The encroachment of the coercive state coupled with an insistence on a disaggregated self-managing (or self-disciplining) workforce leading to poles of overwork and underwork: if this only unevenly applies to automobile manufacture in the 21st century, it seems to perfectly emblematize the production of culture.

Indeed, when it comes to post-Fordist techniques, the culture industries got there first. As Michael Storper illustrates, the film industry had switched to subcontracting in the 1950s: Hollywood "established a putting-out system for pre-production work, in an effort to encourage innovative ideas" (206). The star system was an early version of human capital. The industry has practiced subcontracting, outsourcing, and flexible specialization since the early 1970s. Importantly, as Hollywood's rate of profit fell, studios increasingly had to rely on their film archives as a revenue source. The importance of intellectual property to post-Fordist-neoliberal capitalism was established early on in the production and selling of culture.

The music industry undertook similar experiments in the 1960s, where producers and musicians achieved a greater degree of independence, and eventually small labels began to act as subcontractors for larger ones. Small labels could expand into new markets and share profits with large labels via distribution deals, as large conglomerates held a near-monopoly on distribution (Hesmondhalgh, "Flexibility, Post-Fordism, and the Music Industries" 479–81).

The cultural industries have also acted to interpellate laborers as entrepreneurs. As Neff, Wissinger, and Zukin point out,

> Entrepreneurial labor is not completely new in the culture industries. Since the 1970s, collaborative projects in the film industry have increased the importance of individual, rather than craft-based, skills.

Recognition of these skills comes in the form of 'a piece of the action,' or property rights in the product being developed, in addition to wages. (309)

And further, cultural labor sets the standards for labor in general. As Angela McRobbie, one of the most perceptive commentators on this trend, remarks, "The 'post-industrial' economy is increasingly a 'cultural' economy – with the very understanding of culture itself being appropriated by the enlarged provision of (and longing for) meaningful 'experience'" ("Everyone is Creative"). The cultural economy is how policymakers reconcile the flight from the factory with the decline in stability associated with deindustrialization. "[The government] sees the arts and culture, and the new patterns of freelance work and self-employment associated with being an artist, becoming a model for how economic growth is to be pursued" (ibid). This is the instantiation of capital's response to the crisis in Fordism at the level of industrial policy: to leverage the aesthetic critique of capitalism as a motor of development.

These creative pursuits come with a cost: the requirements to increasingly submit to neoliberal dictates. Creative workers are self-employed, literal entrepreneurs of the self who vend their capacities, their human capital to others. Such a situation lends itself to extreme flexibility: elsewhere, McRobbie notes that "these freelance careers, or the experience of being a small scale entrepreneur, seem to be characterised by constant change: even within the space of a year or two many of these young women will be doing something quite different" ("Reflections" 72). As Neff, Wissinger, and Zukin remark,

> The new economy's cutting edge – and its true social innovation – is the production of a new labor force that is more 'entrepreneurial' than previous generations of workers. This entrepreneurial workforce is risk-taking rather than risk-averse and willing to accept more flexibility in both jobs and careers than workers have been. (309)

Andrew Ross, in his discussion of the precarity of cultural work,[2] underscores this point:

> As paradigms of entrepreneurial selfhood, "creatives," as they are now labeled, are the apple of the policymaker's eye, and recipients of the kind of lip service usually bestowed by national managers on high-tech engineers as generators of value. Art products are the object of intense financial speculation; cultural production is

a top hit-maker in the new jackpot economy; "cultural districts" posited as the key to urban prosperity; and creative industries policy is embraced as the anchor of regional development by governments around the world. In the business world, creativity is viewed as a wonder stuff transforming workplaces into powerhouses of value, while *intellectual property* – the lucrative prize of creative endeavor – is increasingly regarded as the "oil of the 21st century." (32, emphasis mine)

A workforce which is entrepreneurial without being entrepreneurs: as the fruits of their production, in the form of intellectual property, are often expropriated in whole or part from them, cultural workers emerge as a variegated workforce strewn between the poles of the petty bourgeois and the proletarian, and increasingly subject to informal, flexible relations. Here are the central contradictions of the new creative labor force. They achieve a kind of freedom, but only at the expense of security, and the new pressures from this precarity erect new, more insidious, forms of discipline that appear to originate from the self. And, ultimately, while interpellated by media, government, and employers as owners, often the intellectual properties produced by this cultural labor end up in the hands of capital. These contradictions will overdetermine the kinds of struggles over intellectual property and media work described in the following chapters.

Notes

1 Federico Gambino points out that Fordism itself was full of contingency: it was never universally applied, and "post-Fordist" elements such as Toyota's flexible production lines and just-in-time production techniques existed during the "Fordist" period. See "A Critique of the Fordism of the Regulation School." *Common Sense* 19 (June 1996): 42–63.
2 There is much overlap in the conditions of what developmental economists and sociologists describe as the "informal economy" and what commentators have dubbed "precarious" among white-collar workers in the overdeveloped world.

Works Cited

Althusser, Louis. *For Marx*. Trans. Ben Brewster. London: Verso, 2005.
Bologna, Sergio. "Class Composition and the Theory of the Party at the Origin of the Workers-Council Movement." *Telos* 13 (1972): 4–27.
Bourdieu, Pierre. "The Essence of Neoliberalism." *Le Monde Diplomatique*. Dec. 1998. Web. 22 Apr. 2015.
Brenner, Robert. *The Economics of Global Turbulence*. New York, NY: Verso, 2006. Print.

Brown, Wendy. "Neo-liberalism and the End of Liberal Democracy." *Theory & Event* 7.1 (2003). n. pag. Web. 14 June 2014.

Caffentzis, George. *From Capitalist Crises to Proletarian Slavery: An Introduction to Class Struggle in the US, 1973–1998.* Jamaica Plain, MA: G. Caffentzis, 1998.

Castells, Manuel. *The Rise of the Network Society.* Chichester: Wiley-Blackwell, 2010.

Castells, Manuel and Alejandro Portes. "World Underneath: The Origins, Dynamics, and Effects of the Informal Economy." *The Informal Economy: Studies in Advances and Less Developed Countries.* Eds. Manuel Castells, Alejandro Portes, and Lauren A. Benton. Baltimore, MD: The Johns Hopkins UP, 1989. 11–40.

Chatterjee, Partha. "Subaltern Studies and Capital." *Economic and Political Weekly* 48.37 (2013): 69–75.

Chiapello, Eve and Luc Boltanski. *The New Spirit of Capitalism.* Trans. Gregory Elliott. London: Verso, 2007.

Cleaver, Harry. *Reading Capital Politically.* London: AK P, 2000.Dalla Costa, Maria and Selma James. *The Power of Women and the Subversion of the Community.* 2rd ed. London: Falling Wall P, 1973.

Danielzyk, Ranier and Jürgen Ossenbruegge. "Regulation Theory." *International Encyclopedia of the Social and Behavioral Sciences.* Eds. S. Hanson et al. New York, NY: Elsevier, 2001. n. pag. Web. 14 June 2014.

de Soto, Hernando. *The Other Path.* New York: Basic Books, 1989.

Drucker, Peter. *The Age of Discontinuity: Guidelines to Our Changing Society.* London: William Heinemen Ltd, 1970.

Duménil, Gerard and Dominique Lévy. *Capital Resurgent: Roots of the Neoliberal Revolution.* Trans. Derek Jeffers. Cambridge, MA: Harvard UP, 2004.

Dyer-Witheford, Nick. *Cyber-Marx: Cycles and Circuits of Struggle in High-Technology Capitalism.* Champaign/Urbana: U of Illinois P, 1999.

Foucault, Michel. *The Birth of Bio-Politics: Lectures at the Collége de France 1978–1979.* Ed. Michel Senellart. Trans. Graham Burchell. New York, NY: Picador, 2008.

Frow, John. "Information as Gift and Commodity." *New Left Review* No. 219 (Sept.–Oct. 1996): 89–108.

Gambino, Ferruccio. "A Critique of the Fordism of the Regulation School." *Common Sense* 19 (June 1996): 42–63.

Gill, Rosalind C. and Andy Pratt. "In the Social Factory? Immaterial Labour, Precariousness and Cultural Work." *Theory Culture & Society* 25.7–8 (2008): 1–30.

Gramsci, Antonio. *Selections from the Prison Notebooks.* Trans. Quentin Hoare. New York, NY: International Publishers Co., 1971.

Hardt, Michael and Antonio Negri. *Empire.* Cambridge: Harvard UP, 2000.

Harvey, David. *A Brief History of Neoliberalism.* Oxford: Oxford UP, 2005.

———. *The Condition of Postmodernity.* Oxford: Basil Blackwell, 1990.

Harrison, Bennett. *Lean and Mean: Why Large Corporations Will Continue to Dominate the Global Economy.* New York, NY: The Guilford P, 1997.

Heinrich, Michael. "Crisis Theory, the Law of the Tendency of the Profit Rate to Fall, and Marx's Studies in the 1870s." *Monthly Review* 64.11 (Apr. 2003): n. pag. Web. 22 Apr. 2015.

Hesmondhalgh, David. "Flexibility, Post-Fordism and the Music Industries." *Media, Culture and Society* 18 (1996): 469–488.

———. "Neoliberalism, Imperialism, and the Media." *The Media and Social Theory*. Eds. David Hesmondhalgh and Jason Toynbee. London: Routledge, 2008. 95–111.—. "Introduction." *Zerowork: Political Materials* 1 (Dec. 1975): 1–6.

Jessop, Bob. "Liberalism, Neoliberalism, and Urban Governance: A State-Theoretical Perspective." *Antipode* 34.3 (July 2002): 452–472. Web. 14 June 2014.

———. "The State and the Contradictions of the Knowledge-Driven Economy." *Knowledge, Space, Economy*. Eds. John R. Bryson, Peter W. Daniels, Nick D. Henry, and Jane Pollard. London: Routledge, 2000. 63–78.

———. "What Follows Fordism? On the Periodization of Capitalism and Its Regulation." *Phases of Capitalist Development: Booms, Crises, and Globalization*. Eds. Robert Albritton et al. Basingstoke: Palgrave, 2001. 282–299.

Lash, Scott and John Urry. *The End of Organized Capitalism*. Madison: U of Wisconsin P, 1987.

Lipietz, Alain. "Towards Global Fordism?" *New Left Review* No. 132 (Mar.–Apr. 1982): 33–47.

Mandel, Ernst. *Late Capitalism*. London: Verso, 1999.

Marx, Karl. *Capital: A Critique of Political Economy, Volume 3*. Trans. David Fernbach. London: Penguin Books, 1993.

———. "The German Ideology." *Selected Writings*. 2nd ed. Ed. David McLellan. Oxford: Oxford UP, 2006. 175–208.

———. *Theories of Surplus Value, Part I*. Moscow: Progress Publishers, 1978.

McRobbie, Angela. "'Everyone Is Creative': Artists as New Economy Pioneers?" *Open Democracy*. 30 Aug. 2001. Web. 14 June 2014.

———. "Reflections on Feminism, Immaterial Labour and the Post-Fordist Regime." *New Formations* 70.17 (Winter 2011): 60–76.

Miller, Toby, et al. *Global Hollywood 2*. New York, NY: Bloomsbury, 2004.

Mirowski, Philip. *Never Let a Serious Crisis Go to Waste: How Neoliberalism Survived the Financial Meltdown*. London: Verso, 2013.

———. "Postface: Defining Neoliberalism." *The Road from Mont Pélerin: The Making of the Neoliberal Thought Collective*. Eds. Philip Mirowski and Dieter Plehwe. Cambridge: Harvard UP, 2009. 417–455.

Moody, Kim. *Workers in a Lean World: Unions in the International Economy*. New York, NY: Verso, 1997.

Moseley, Fred. *The Falling Rate of Profit in the Postwar United States Economy*. Basingstoke: Palgrave Macmillan, 1991.

Neff, Gina, Elizabeth Wissinger, and Sharon Zukin. "Entrepreneurial Labor among Cultural Producers: 'Cool' Jobs in 'Hot' Industries." *Social Semiotics* 15.3 (December 2005): 307–334.

Negri, Toni. "Archaeology and Project: The Mass Worker and the Social Worker." *Common Sense* 3 (1987): 43–71.

Neuwirth, Robert. *The Stealth of Nations: The Global Rise of the Informal Economy.* New York, NY: Anchor, 2011.

Ong, Aiwha. *Neoliberalism as Exception: Mutations in Citizenship and Sovereignty.* Durham, NC: Duke UP, 2006.

Peck, Jamie and Adam Tickell. "Searching for a New Institutional Fix: the After-Fordist Crisis and the Global-Local Disorder." *Post-Fordism: A Reader.* Ed. Ash Amin. Oxford: Blackwell, 1995. 280–315.

Ross, Andrew. *No-Collar: The Humane Workplace and Its Hidden Costs.* New York, NY: Basic Books, 2003.

Sassen-Koob, Saskia. "New York's Informal Economy." *The Informal Economy: Studies in Advances and Less Developed Countries.* Eds. Alejandro Portes, Manuel Castells, and Lauren A. Benton. Baltimore, MD: The Johns Hopkins UP, 1989. 60–77.

Smith, Tony. *Technology and Capital in the Age of Lean Production: A Marxian Critique of the "New Economy."* Albany: State U of New York P, 2003.

Storper, Michael. "The Transition to Flexible Specialisation in the US Film Industry: External Economies, the Division of Labour and the Crossing of Industrial Divides." *Post-Fordism: A Reader.* Ed. Ash Amin. Oxford: Blackwell, 1995. 195–226.

Tomaney, John. "A New Paradigm of Work Organization and Technology?" *Post-Fordism: A Reader.* Ed. Ash Amin. Oxford: Blackwell, 1995. 157–194.

Tronti, Mario. "Lenin in England." *Marxists Internet Archive.* n.d. Web. 12 June 2014.

Wacquant, Loïc. "Three Steps to a Historical Anthropology of Actually Existing Neoliberalism." *Social Anthropology* 20.1 (2012): 66–79.

Wallerstein, Immanuel. *Historical Capitalism with Capitalist Civilization.* London: Verso, 1996.

2 The Critique of the Digital Political Economy

As detailed in the previous chapter, post-Fordist-neoliberal restructuring altered labor processes of workers by making them "flexible" and "precarious" and "creative." It also globalized labor through subcontracting, a process requiring large investments in communications and information technology infrastructure, as well as enhancing intellectual property rights.

The labor required to produce this infrastructure contained its own contradictions. Struggles broke out over the ways the work of developing this new IT infrastructure would progress, often involving the question of intellectual property. Related struggles emerged over intellectual property and cultural production, which increasingly took the recombinant form usefully described by art critic Nicolas Bourriard as "post-production": the creation of works by the reordering and recontextualization of existing cultural artifacts, often through the use of digital tools. These struggles were shaped by a vanguard of skilled computer users, often described as "hackers."

This chapter will examine struggles over intellectual property in digital space as labor struggles within the context of capitalist restructuring. These struggles attempted to intervene in the process of recomposing the decomposed working classes of Fordism, bringing their practices and ideologies to bear. I will begin by describing the resistance by early computer programmers and hackers to intellectual property laws as a conflict over autonomy and working conditions.

I will then examine the influential body of work over "copyfight," the struggle over the role of intellectual property and cultural work in the new economy. Commentators in this vein (to a great extent, technologically adept US Americans trained as lawyers) celebrate the potentials of a new mode of production, while representing conflicts over copyright as primarily about the civil liberties of computer users. In doing so, they tend to neglect or mystify the role of labor as a source of antagonism.

I will then move to examining two bodies of thought examining cultural labor and digital technology from a Marxist perspective. The first, the cognitive capitalist school, derives much of its vocabulary from autonomist analysis and revolves around theorizing digitally mediated production as "immaterial labor." Immaterial labor reveals a host of new radical potentials for the working class, though this analysis tends to depart from Marxist analysis in important ways. The second, which I group together as "digital labor," hews much more closely to Marx's fundamental concepts and offers a better theorization of the ambiguous position of piracy in digital capitalism.

Hacker Culture

In explaining how intellectual property, specifically copyright, became a flashpoint of antagonism in digital culture, it is difficult not to reach for technologically determinist explanations. A computer is a kind of copying machine, where digital information, encoded in the ones and zeros of binary code, are easy to copy. Second, networked computers essentially automate this copying process in the transfer of information. The language of "transfer" of "packets" obscures the fact that digital artifacts are not moved from computer to computer so much as assembled on the spot. The ease by which computers copy information is not a side effect, but an essential component of the power of networked computers; as the saying goes, a feature, not a bug.

But there is more to the story of intellectual property conflicts than the inherent capabilities of digital technology. Those technological capabilities were realized in human practice that was organized in specific ways, and within specific contexts. Without including the meaningful organization of human practice – in short, culture – the story of copyright and piracy lacks its protagonist. This organization first takes root in the dawn of software programming.

In the early days of computing and programming, software was not a commodity. Computer hardware itself was the chief commodity, an immense capital investment which only large firms, the military, and universities could afford. These institutions relied upon skilled technicians to develop programs particular to the computer and the tasks required of it. Much of the research behind computer programming occurred in university computer science departments, insulated from the concerns of business and commerce. Because software was laborious to produce and not considered a commercial prospect, a culture of sharing code developed among programmers, a group which included university computer scientists and graduate students as well as various amateur tinkerers without direct university affiliation. As Richard Stallman, who would later found the Free Software movement, describes his experience, "When I started working at the MIT Artificial Intelligence Lab in 1971, I became part of a software-sharing community that had existed for many years" (17). For Stallman, the free sharing of software and code was an essential part of programming:

> Sharing of software was not limited to our particular community; it is as old as computers, just as sharing of recipes is as old as cooking.... Whenever people from another university or a company wanted to port and use a program, we gladly let them. If you saw someone using an unfamiliar and interesting program, you could always ask to see the source code, so that you could read it, change it, or cannibalize parts of it to make a new program. (ibid)

These sharing communities were one of the origins of the computer-based subculture of hackers.

As personal computing grew, so did the market for software, leading to an emergence of a commercial software industry. However, the hobbyist clubs from which the personal computer (PC) industry would emerge shared Stallman's hacker values and practices: the ability to test, deconstruct, learn from, and share software, primarily as a means to build skills in programming and computer networking. Providing other hobbyists with a disk of copied software free of charge was a common practice; club members often taught themselves programming by collaboratively deconstructing software. These activities did not go unnoticed by the nascent commercial software industry, concerned about creating stable markets for their commodities. Bill Gates's infamous 1976 letter excoriating the PC hobbyists who shared his young company's Altair BASIC program harshly condemned such practices: "most of you steal your software. Hardware must be paid for, but software is something to share. Who cares if the people who worked on it get paid?"

Gates, along with his company Microsoft, would emerge as the bête noire of what Douglas Thomas describes as the second generation of hacker culture. Unlike the university hackers, the second generation emerged in the personal computing era, as computers became consumer products and home appliances rather than fixed capital investments. Hacker culture, as Thomas characterizes it, is

> a culture that expressed a general dissatisfaction with the world, typical of teenage angst, but also a dissatisfaction with ways technology was being used. For teenage boys discovering the ways

that computers could be used to reach out to one another, there was nothing more disturbing than seeing those same computers being used to systematically organize the world. Groups of hackers began to meet, to learn from one another, and to form a subculture, which was dedicated to resisting and interrupting "the system." (xii)

Intellectual property restrictions against sharing code and programs made up a part of that "system" (to be discussed more extensively in the next chapter), but Thomas also points to the "world of passwords and PIN numbers" (xi) governed by large institutions, such as the military, the government, and large corporations, which threatened hackers' freedom of movement and access within digital networks.

Gilles Deleuze offers a suggestive description of this world. He argues that the era of disciplinary institutions theorized by Michel Foucault, which served to create an industrial labor force at the moment of enclosure, has given way to "societies of control." According to Deleuze, as disciplinary institutions, responsible for producing discrete subjects such as "soldier" or "worker" break down, people are increasingly subject to a kind of free-floating domination, "postponements" of "continuous variation" enforced by passwords: "codes that mark access to information, or reject it" (5). These are the forms of control over the social factory discussed in the previous chapter, where production and reproduction extend beyond "enclosures" into "circuits" (6): control relies upon access and credentialing, and capitalist production tends toward the immaterial. Crucially, "societies of control operate with machines of a third type, computers, whose passive danger is jamming and whose active one is piracy and the introduction of viruses" (ibid).

Deleuze points to the transition point between Fordism and post-Fordism, though not in those terms. Institutions disaggregate as the workforce is decomposed into more atomized and flexible subjectivities. Access to credentials and passwords requires the workforce to recompose along neoliberal lines, acquiring the proper human capital and investments in one's self to increase one's autonomy. What we shall see are the practices developed within hacker culture to resist the control society, as well as the commodification of personal computing. Instead, hackers constructed alternate methods of traversing networks, interacting online, and exchanging information. The totality of these practices and networks became known as the computer underground.

The work of Cornelius Castoriadis contains a pertinent theoretical framework for the computer underground. A factory worker himself, and a fierce critic of despotic management techniques, Castoriadis argued that capitalist control of the process of production could, in fact, never be complete. All management, even the extremely detailed directives of bodies and motion developed by the "scientific management" of Frederick Winslow Taylor and his disciples, had to be instituted at the level of a plan, the execution of which had to involve some modicum of worker agency. Further, plans had to be implemented in diverse settings, requiring all manner of modifications, fixes, and adaptations. "The 'one best way' has no relation to the concrete reality of production. Its definition presupposes the existence of ideal conditions, conditions that are extremely far removed from the actual conditions the worker faces" (161). Even in the face of Taylorism, workers practiced a kind of self-management, which was, for Castoriadis, the kernel of socialist relations.

The totality of these self-management practices constitutes the "informal organization of the enterprise": the actually existing manifestation of productive practice, which for Castoriadis, possesses "a social content, a content having to do with struggle" (170). Rather than emerging in the aporias of technocratic dominance, as in Michel de Certeau's theorization of tactics: "a calculated action determined by the absence of a proper locus" (37), informal organization confronts the formal plans of management:

> The informal organization is not an excrescence appearing in the interstices of the formal organization; it tends to represent a different mode of operation of the enterprise, centred around the real situation of the executants. The direction, the dynamic, and the outlook of the two organizations are entirely opposite – and opposed on a social terrain that ultimately coincides with that of the struggle between directors and executants. (171)

As control mechanisms – passcodes, firewalls, copy protections – were introduced throughout the new productive forces of computer networks, just such informal organizations arose to contest them, to attempt alternative ways to recompose the working classes, starting with those who worked with computers.

Free Software

As the PC industry grew, with the software industry growing alongside it, hackers ran up against challenges to the self-management of their computer activity. The sharing of software code had been ruled, in a somewhat curious 1978 Supreme Court decision, illegal. While the court decided algorithms could not be patented, it ruled that pieces of computer code, as expressions of underlying ideas of how best to craft software, are protected by copyright. This had two notable effects. First, US copyright protections are automatic: unlike patents, which must be registered with the US Patent Office, "[t]he law automatically protects a work that is created and fixed in a tangible medium of expression on or after January 1, 1978." As soon as code was written, it became intellectual property. Second, copyright protections last an extremely long time: while patents expire after 20 years, copyright endures for the author's lifetime plus 70 years, or, for anonymous works, 120 years from the moment of creation.

The consequences were immediately clear to computer programmers. Sharing of code, a fundamental component of the work of programming and hacking, would be illegal. In response, Stallman formed a special-interest group, the Free Software Foundation, and designed a novel licensing scheme to use as an alternative to copyright for his programming. Stallman's goal for the GNU General Public Licenses, or "copyleft," was the preservation of the labor practices he enjoyed as a computer scientist at the Massachusetts Institute of Technology (MIT), where, insulated from capitalist pressures of profit maximization, he enjoyed a great deal of autonomy.

> Our General Public Licenses are designed to make sure that you have the freedom to distribute copies of free software (and charge for them if you wish), that you receive source code or can get it if you want it, that you can change the software or use pieces of it in new free programs, and that you know you can do these things. ("Gnu Project – Free Software Foundation")

In what Coleman and Hill call a "clever legal hack" (515), the General Public License (GPL) effectively uses the ironclad law of copyright licensing to require anyone who builds programs from free software to share source code, removing the ability for anyone to monopolize their programs. As Stallman puts it, "Copyleft uses copyright law, but flips it over to serve the opposite of its usual purpose: instead of a means of privatizing software, it becomes a means of keeping software free" (22). Stallman's initiative quickly captured the imagination of programmers connected to the computer underground, whose members set to work building a software ecosystem unrestricted by copyright.

Dafermos and Söderberg have argued that free software hacker politics should be understood as a kind of labor struggle against management, as well as a flight from corporate existence:

> In attempting to escape from alienated existence, the hacker movement has invented an alternative model for organising labour founded on the common ownership of the means of production, on volunteer participation and the principle of self-expression in work. It is this promise that lies at the heart of the politics of the hacker movement. (54)

In other words, this movement takes the form of an informal organization as described by Castoriadis, an alternative form of productive relationships, existing parallel to the capitalist management of the Internet. Rather than explicitly anti-capitalist, hacker politics emerge from hackers' resistance to the ways that capital attempted to intervene and control their work processes through intellectual property. The GPL allowed hackers to retain a measure of undisciplined and nonroutine autonomy, what Dafermos and Söderberg refer to as the hacker "rejection of Taylorism" (56). Hackers seek to maintain their skill and independence in the face of tendencies to deskill and control the production of software inside large firms.

The free software movement's biggest success was the development of the operating system Linux. Linus Torvalds, a Finnish computer science student, used an online newsgroup to solicit assistance in programming a free operating system. Hundreds of individuals volunteered unpaid time to build pieces of code for the project, which eventually became a fully functioning operating system designed according to Free Software principles. The success of Linux proved that the distributed free software organization, in spite of its chaotic appearance, represented a viable model for software development, miles away from corporate strategies. But it represented more than this. Through harnessing a dispersed group of volunteers, organized for a cause rather than through wages and management structures, free software represented an alternative mode of production and a new kind of democratic organization, a concrete apotheosis of the political and economic revolution that had been the promise of personal computing from its earliest days. The triumph of an unpaid network-based community of programmers creating a free and open product in the face of the intellectual-property-dependent monopoly like Microsoft seemed to herald Marx's prophetic statement in *Contribution to the Critique of Political Economy*:

At a certain stage of development, the material productive forces of society come into conflict with the existing relations of production or – this merely expresses the same thing in legal terms – with the property relations within the framework of which they have operated hitherto. From forms of development of the productive forces these relations turn into their fetters. Then begins an era of social revolution. The changes in the economic foundation lead sooner or later to the transformation of the whole immense superstructure.

This passage sees Marx at his most technologically determinist. The material productive forces develop in ways that undermine existing political structures, which begin to impede development. This contradiction is resolved in revolution. Applied to code, Marx could be discussing how intellectual property became a fetter on software development, until free software finally put it asunder.

Political economist Yochai Benkler attempts just such an ambitious analysis in the massively influential *Wealth of Networks* (alluding to Adam Smith, rather than Marx). For Benkler, projects like Linux are an example of an emergent mode of production, what he calls "commons-based peer production." Such production is characterized by "cooperative and coordinate action carried out through radically distributed, nonmarket mechanisms that do not depend on proprietary strategies" (3). If, rather than intellectual property rights restricting access to code and information, the digital world is instead treated as a commons, users can make small contributions in their free time, which coalesce into large projects. Free and open-source software are, for Benkler, the paradigmatic examples: tools, such as the Linux operating system, can be created by the joint efforts of thousands without the need for compensation or future commodification.

The existence of voluntary, autonomous work captured imaginations such as Benkler's for a simple reason: it made apparent what Marxists have always emphasized, the social character of labor. Bereft of wage labor, and producing non-commodified objects, the mechanics of commodity fetishism, by which "the commodity reflects the social characteristics of men's own labour as objective characteristics of the product of labour themselves," does not take hold (*Capital Volume 1* 164–5).

Under commodity production, "producers do not come into social contact with each other until they exchange the products of their labour," and so "the specific social character of their private labours appear only within this exchange" (165). However, without mediation from wages and the market, the commodity fetish falls apart, and labor appears as social, rather than individual.

Further, for nonmarket-based products such as free software, in which use rather than exchange is paramount, the social relations of commodity society are denaturalized. Workers are better able to imagine arrangements of productive work alternative to capitalist wage labor; as Bollier describes it, "commoners are more intent on building a kind of parallel social order, inscribed within the regnant political economy but animated by their own values" (9). Many analyses (such as McKenzie Wark's *Hacker Manifesto*) express these values as an enthusiasm for online "gift economies," a response to the falling veil of commodity fetishism.

And yet, free software as a productive process hasn't fully escaped capitalist social relations. For one, capitalism has always relied upon forms of labor that appear outside the wage. Marxist feminists such as Maria Dalla Costa, Selma James, and Sylvia Federici have demonstrated how the reproduction of capitalist relations relies on the unpaid reproductive labor of women within the family and the home. Furthermore, for all its radical ambitions, free software was never entirely antagonistic to capitalism. Business came to recognize the advantages of what libertarian programmer Eric Raymond called "the bazaar" of dispersed nonproprietary coding, as opposed to hierarchical "cathedral" of strong IP protections: better products produced more cheaply. Seeking to mollify capitalists concerned about the implications of the word "free" attached to their products, entrepreneurs Bruce Perens and Tim O'Reilly rebranded the movement as "open source" to encourage investment. The ploy worked. As Bollier documents, International Business Machines (IBM) spent $1 billion on Linux development; companies such as Amazon and eBay converted to open source, and as of 2002, "[a]s many as one-third of the programmers working on open-source projects are corporate employees" (38). In addition to its niche as an operating system for individual computer users, Linux is now a component of the majority of servers, routers, and supercomputers: in other words, it is a vital element of the infrastructure of the Internet. Just as capitalism relies on public infrastructure such as roads, or common spaces, such as international waterways, in order to produce and distribute commodities, so too does it rely on free and open-source software.

Free Culture and Creative Commons

The successes of the Free Software movement subsequently inspired challenges to copyright in the cultural realm. The culture industries, which had already begun the process of digitizing their properties to cheapen production and distribution, were alarmed by the ways in which digital technology allowed users to copy, rearrange, and remix their brands, trademarks, and goods. Potent artistic techniques, such as pastiche, collage, remix, and détournement, developed in 20th century as a response to mass production, were rendered simple by digitalization and computers, and became cornerstones of contemporary creative practice (Bourriard, Coombe).

Eager to secure their existing hegemony of distribution in the face of technologies and cultural practices that enshrined grassroots copying and distributing of information, the cultural industries attempted to impose strict copyright over media content on the web. A National Information Infrastructure white paper on digital copyright became the Digital Millennium Copyright Act of 1998, which clarified IP protections online and criminalized circumvention of copy protections.

In response to these measures, a reform movement arose, led by law professors, such as Lawrence Lessig, and online civil liberties organizations, such as the Electronic Frontier Foundation: the Free Culture movement (Bollier 42–68). Following Stallman's example, the Free Culture movement started an organization, Creative Commons, to create and administer alternative licenses, which would modify copyright, permitting reuse, remixing, and sharing of digital content. In what follows, I will document through a close reading of its foundational texts how the Free Culture movement embodies a politically liberal initiative in its understanding of conflicts over digital culture and in its methods and goals for amelioration.

Lessig's 2004 manifesto for the movement, *Free Culture*, lays out in plain language and colorful anecdotes the major values of the Free Culture movement. While Lessig is overt that the movement is directly inspired by Stallman's Free Software Foundation's work, he breaks with Stallman along important lines. Where Stallman concerned himself with the working conditions of software programming, albeit expressed in terms of individual freedom, Lessig orients his criticism of copyright toward its effects on civil liberties, specifically freedom of speech. For Lessig, creating, manipulating, and distributing cultural works is a "form of speech" (40), and the Internet is likened to film photography as a "democratic technology of expression" (35). As speech, the circulation of these artifacts must be protected from government intervention.

In making this argument, Lessig deliberately collapses the categories of cultural commodities with those of speech. The ease of digital production and distribution has transformed works governed by property rights – photographs, music, films – into new varieties of individual speech. But rather than rely purely on First Amendment rights to freedom of speech, Lessig appeals to the ideology of free market competition, treating digital content as a hybrid form, a kind of speech-commodity. "It is always a bad deal for the government to get into the business of regulating speech markets" (128). Echoing libertarian economist Friedrich Hayek, Lessig argues that state enforcement of copyright is an ill-advised interference in the market of speech and ideas, a road to serfdom leading to economic decline and political repression. "A world in which competitors with new ideas must fight not only the market but also the government is a world in which competitors with new ideas will not succeed. It is a world of stasis and increasingly concentrated stagnation. It is the Soviet Union under Brezhnev" (ibid). Lessig's argument also recalls economist Joseph Schumpeter by valorizing the creative destruction of existing cultural industries to the benefit of innovators. Intellectual property law is an instance of "[o]verregulation [which] stifles creativity. It smothers innovation. It gives dinosaurs [media industries] a veto over the future. It wastes the extraordinary opportunity for a democratic creativity that digital technology enables" (199).

Reframing the Free Software movement's concerns with working conditions as concerns over free speech that are deeply imbricated with the dynamics of markets demonstrates Free Culture's debt to liberal, and even libertarian, terms of debate. In doing so, it mimics the Supreme Court's own curious logic that deemed computer code, typically a commodity, a creative expression. Many scholars of free software follow this logic, focusing on its expressive elements, rather than its status as a form of work under capitalism. Chris Kelty imagines free software development as a liberal public sphere, referring to the "recursive public of geeks" who craft a "moral-technical order" of openness and freedom (145, 187). Coleman and Golub argue that "the language that hackers frequently invoke to describe themselves or formulate ethical claims – freedom, free speech, privacy, the individual, meritocracy – discloses liberal imprints and concerns" (256), though they later reveal a more Nietzschean side to hackers, who revel in "their ability to play with legal boundaries" (265). While elsewhere Coleman suggests hacking is about control over work – "Freedom [for hackers] is understood foremost to be about personal control and autonomous production" – she maintains that hackers subscribe to a political liberalism grounded in civil liberties ("Code Is Speech" 428).

Just as Stallman developed alternative licenses to subvert intellectual property protections, so too did Lessig and the Free Culture movement. Creative Commons' "aim is to build a layer of reasonable copyright on top of the extremes that now reign. It does this by making it easy for people to build upon other people's work, by making it simple for creators to express the freedom for others to take and build upon their work" (282). With a Creative Commons license, copyright holders voluntarily relinquish some rights over the media they create, allowing others to redistribute or remix their work. While there is variation, most Creative-Commons-licensed objects require that authorial credit be retained, and typically restrict profit-making for all but the original creator.

The name "Creative Commons" provides a path toward understanding the ideology behind it. In the first decade of the 21st century, the idea of digital content as a "commons" was exceedingly influential. Law professor James Boyle's *Public Domain: Enclosing the Commons of the Mind* provides a detailed excavation of the concept, in terms designed for their relevance in the fight for copyright reform. Boyle begins by describing copyright as a kind of liberal legal innovation designed to balance competing interests: an "attempt to use a legally created privilege to solve a potential 'public goods problem'" of incentivizing innovation while also assuring the benefits of those innovations would spread throughout society (8). Arguing that "the goal of the system ought to be to give the monopoly only for as long as necessary to provide an incentive" (11), Boyle enlists a host of liberal figures, including Adam Smith, Thomas Jefferson, and Thomas Babington Macaulay, all of whom "could see good reason why intellectual property rights should be granted. They simply insisted on weighing the costs and benefits of a new right, each expansion of scope, each lengthening of the copyright term" (23). The public domain, encompassing works whose rights have expired, as well as protected uses, such as fair use, consists of "reserved spaces of freedom inside intellectual property" (38). These reservations are, ideally, protected by a state adhering to the spirit of the Patent and Copyright clause of the US Constitution: "To promote the Progress of Science and useful Arts, by securing for limited Times to Authors and Inventors the exclusive Right to their respective Writings and Discoveries." The point is to reform copyright to create a commons/public domain from which further innovations can be produced.

The commons acts as a kind of regulatory ideal for the liberal reformists such as Boyle and Lessig. It replaces the liberal public sphere of free expression with a metaphor more suited for the free (albeit with some restrictions) circulation of commodities. It is also a powerful political metaphor, aligning hackers and IP reformers with the historical social movements documented by E.P. Thompson, Marcus Rediker, and Peter Linebaugh, who illustrate that "pirate" and "outlaw" were terms meant to diminish the resistance to 18th-century land enclosures and the new capitalist relations they imposed. Boyle overtly signals to this history by describing copyright as a "new enclosure movement."

Historically, however, resistance to enclosures was not merely about access to property. It was also an attack on new labor relations. Separation from the commons was a precondition for restructuring the labor process away from feudal craft techniques and toward deskilled wage labor in factories. Thompson chronicles not only opposition to private property in defense of commons, but also a defense of craft labor practices. Periodically, groups of workers destroyed the fences blocking their access to grazing land, and attacked the machines that had mechanized their jobs and destroyed their livelihoods. In Rediker's account of Atlantic piracy of the same time period, piracy's appeal to sailors is one of democratic working conditions and profit-sharing, as opposed to the exploitative and hierarchical organization of merchant and military vessels. However, like Lessig, Boyle buries history of labor struggles against enclosure, favoring appeals to public good and civil liberties.

"Creative" is also word that performs a great deal of work for many social reformers of the neoliberal era, including Lessig, and like the slanted appeal to the commons, also works to mystify the contentious labor relations at the heart of digital culture. One the one hand, it is intimately tied up with labor, as in John Howkins' "creative economy" and Richard Florida's "creative class," which view new varieties of cultural work as bringing about improved social relations. But, because it is also linked to notions of artistic practice and authorship, it also carries, particularly in Lessig's account, connotations of expressive communication, as well as spontaneity. In this, it mystifies its link to labor. Instead of workers, Lessig confronts his reader with artists, and mostly amateur artists at that, who make their works for fun and self-fulfillment, without a thought for compensation.

While not workers, these creators are indeed owners, as the licenses preserve the authorial role, even while relaxing other elements of the work as private property. As Dmytri Kleiner puts it in his critique of Creative Commons,

> Creative Commons exists to help "you," the producer, keep control of "your" work. You are invited to choose from among a range of restrictions you wish to apply to "your" work, such as forbidding duplication, forbidding derivative works, or forbidding commercial use. It is assumed that, as an author-producer, everything you make and everything you say is your property. (34)

This emphasis on the individual creator means that, rhetoric aside, Creative Commons is something very different from free software's expanding world of free code. Creative Commons continues to upholding of the notion of the original author, what Kleiner calls "producer-control." As Foucault describes it, this "author-function" is "a certain functional principle by which, in our culture, one limits, excludes, and chooses; in short, by which one impedes the free circulation, the free manipulation, the free composition, decomposition, and recomposition of fiction" (221). In upholding the author, Creative Commons continues to impede free circulation, manipulation, composition, and recomposition of works. However, rather than make these impediments compulsory and total as with traditional copyright, it reconstructs them as authorial choices, unbundling each of these by constructing new contractual language.

The preservation of authorship has the effect of preserving, in turn, the bourgeois subject upon which copyright rests. As Martha Woodmansee documents, with the rise of the bourgeois class came "the rise in the eighteenth century of a new group of individuals: writers who sought to earn their livelihood from the sale of their writings to the new and rapidly expanding reading public" (426). These bourgeois writers, the creative class of their time, required individual property rights over their works, so that they could subsequently exchange those works on the market. They thus constructed a bourgeois notion of authorship as a private property right located in the expression of ideas.

Authorship does not merely create owners who then assume privileges; it also establishes a particular kind of juridical subject. Governance is a prerequisite for market relations, and capitalism requires specific juridical forms to maintain orderly commodity exchange. As Marxist legal theorist Evgeny Pashukanis describes it, under capitalism

> The legal subject is thus an abstract owner of commodities raised to the heavens. His will in the legal sense has its real basis in the desire to alienate through acquisition and to profit through alienating. For this desire to be fulfilled, it is absolutely essential that the wishes of commodity owners meet each other halfway. This relationship is expressed in legal terms as a contract or an agreement concluded between autonomous wills. Hence the contract is a concept central to law. (121)

For Pashukanis, the law of contract presupposes (or in Althusserian language, interpellates) subjects as abstractly equal individual owners, "subjects of right." The creators envisioned by Creative Commons, full of remixers and documentary filmmakers and mash-up artists, are a new bourgeois-subject-in-becoming, if only copyright laws can be reformed in a way to redraw the line between legitimate and illegitimate uses, via micro-contracts layered on top of existing copyright, thus protecting certain those activities deemed "creative" or "innovative." The juridical subject of Creative Commons, an author and owner, perfectly aligns with the neoliberal subject who is an entrepreneur, rather than a worker. In this way, the liberal reform of intellectual property becomes a vehicle of the neoliberal recomposition of the working class.

Yet contradictions continue to abound in such a project. When, precisely, is violating copyright a permitted activity of a "creative" to be encouraged, and when is it a destructive activity of a "pirate" to be outlawed? As Kavita Philip points out, Free Culture partisans "seek successfully to ground a future consensus on the basis of the exclusion of 'bad' copying, distinguishing illegal sharing from good, creative sharing" (207). The distinction, crucial to the legitimacy of the Free Culture reform movement, is ultimately settled on orientalist lines. Good copying is the activity of an implicitly Western creative class; bad sharing is the activity of what Lessig describes as "businesses" in "Asia and Eastern Europe" "that do nothing but take others people's copyrighted content, copy it, and sell it…. This piracy is wrong" (*Free Culture* 63). As Philip notes,

> Here Lessig is firmly drawing a distinction that, to his consternation, had been commonly blurred in public discussions of the free culture movement. He is particularly concerned to draw this distinction because both his followers and critics often see his advocacy of free culture as flouting the laws of markets and property. Asian pirates thus serve as his limit case: the limit point of difference from bourgeois law, the point toward which the energies unleashed by the free culture/free software movement tend, often, chaotically and euphorically, to move, but the dangerous borders from which it must be turned back, lest the foundations of bourgeois law be threatened. (212)

In the light of Phillips and Pashukanis, Lessig's project takes on à new appearance. His ultimate goal is not a revolution in cultural production, but an attempt to shore up bourgeois law threatened by new technology and new practices which violate private property rights. He attempts this via appending his proposed reforms to a new kind of bourgeois subject: the creative. In fashioning this distinction between creatives and pirates, there is not only a division drawn, as Philip notes, between the West and Asia, but also, corresponding to this division, one between "creative" intellectual labor and labor of other kinds. This distinction is at the heart of the liberal reformist political economy of the digital world.

Free and open-source software programming revealed the socialization of labor mystified by commodity exchange and the contract. It simultaneously constructed a new juridical status alternative to the bourgeois legal subject, where producers relinquish their exclusive right to their creation, along with wages and profits that commodity exchange would entail, effectively giving it away. Creative Commons does something very different. It re-establishes the bourgeois subject in ways that privilege emergent productive processes in the Western middle class in an effort to formalize this kind of labor, establishing a juridical regime of property rights and contracts to control distribution and profit-making. It is a grassroots effort to recompose privileged segments of the vast informal organization of the online social factory.

But what sort of recomposition does the Free Culture movement envision? Here we should return to Benkler's political economy to find answers. In places, Benkler sounds quite Marxist. Echoing Marxist calls for collective ownership of the means of production, Benkler claims that "The material requirements for effective information production and communication are now owned by numbers of individuals several orders of magnitude larger than the number of owners of the basic means of information production and exchange a mere two decades ago" (4). Ownership of PCs is likened to ownership of the means of production, albeit limited to specific realms of production: information, media, and culture. This enthusiasm for a redistribution of production capabilities is emblematic of what Tony Smith calls Benkler's "liberal egalitarian" and "historical materialist" perspective (157).

As egalitarian as this may be in intent, Benkler's work, particularly when applied to a creative class juridical subject as Lessig does, is not digital socialism, but what Marx in Volume 1 of *Capital* calls the "petty mode of production," in which "the labourer is the free proprietor of the conditions of his labour, and sets them in motion himself" (927). This petty bourgeois formation aligns well with the neoliberal entrepreneurial subject, though I want to suggest a specifically US American lineage as well. These rugged individualist creatives subsist on the code and culture they themselves produce, instead of what they get from "top-down" software and media corporations. In this, they closely resemble the yeoman farmer lionized by Thomas Jefferson.

Richard Barbrook and Andy Cameron, in their classic critique of Silicon Valley "The Californian Ideology," remark upon the likeness between hacker culture and Jeffersonian ideals. And, as an outgrowth of hacker culture, the Free Culture movement has similarly made Jefferson an important figure in their lineage. Jefferson generally opposed intellectual property restrictions, leading Boyle to draft him into the Free Culture movement as a fellow traveller who articulated "a skeptical recognition that intellectual property rights might be necessary, a careful explanation that they should not be treated as natural rights, and a warning of the monopolistic dangers that they pose" (21). Lessig cites Jefferson's remarks on intellectual property approvingly in *Free Culture* (84). "Thomas Jefferson and the other Founding Fathers were thoughtful, and got it right," states Kembrew McLeod in his discussion of the US Constitution's clauses on patent and copyright.

Jefferson thought small industrious landholders mobilized republican virtues against aristocracy: "Cultivators of the earth are the most valuable citizens. They are the most vigorous, the most independent, the most virtuous, & they are tied to their country & wedded to it's [sic] liberty & interests by the most lasting bonds" (quoted in Hardt 54). According to Michael Hardt, Jefferson preferred an agricultural economy to a manufacturing one, as "the virtue of agriculture is that this possibility of an equal distribution of property can form the basis of the political equality of independent citizen-producers" (56). For Lessig, a rising class of "geeks" requires free, or at least deregulated, access to media goods – culture – which it can then develop and transform, reshaping politics. "The puzzle that stymies Jefferson is how to create common and equal access to productive property when that property is not simply given by nature but the product of previous social production" (58), a problem Lessig himself tackles explicitly via his legal advocacy and projects such as Creative Commons.

Important for liberalism, as represented by both Jefferson and Lessig, is that a commons is built, and equality is established, without any violation of private property. With the case of Jefferson, the obvious caveat is that his vision explicitly required expropriation and colonization of the Indians. Rather than resuscitate the alleged (and avowedly incoherent) "revolutionary core" of Jefferson's thought, as Hardt seeks to do (57), we might recognize, as Domenico Losurdo extensively articulates in *Liberalism*, how liberal political thought consistently forms a set of exclusions, often racialized, in an effort to protect the property and the rights of expropriation of a privileged class. The digital yeoman farmers, who are hacking, remixing, and creating their own innovations and forms of culture, are the core of the Jeffersonian imagination of the liberal reformers of intellectual property. And this imagination reproduces the contradictions of Jefferson's society by privileging a specific class fragment, and ignoring the rest.

Immaterial Labor and Cognitive Capitalism

It comes as something of a surprise that the liberal Free Culture movement and certain writers from the Marxist *post-operaismo* tendency, such as Michael Hardt, share an affinity for Thomas Jefferson. But there are other affinities as well, in the focus on a particular class fragment borne aloft on a belief in technological revolution. However, first it is necessary to reconstruct the theory of what, for convenience's sake, I will group together as autonomist Marxists.

Autonomist Marxism's approach to the digital economy relies on a reading of Marx's *Grundrisse*. The high concentration of technology at work in the digital economy recalls a passage from Marx's *Grundrisse* that autonomists have pored over for years, the so-called "Fragment on Machines." According to Marx, the development of the productive forces reaches a level in which "it is the machine which possesses skill and strength in place of the worker, is itself the virtuoso" (693). In this arrangement, the worker "merely transmits the machine's work, the machine's action, on to the raw material – supervises it and guards against interruptions" (694).

The introduction of new techniques of automation and digital communication into the productive process during the crisis in Fordism led many autonomists to view the Fragment as an apt description of the new conjuncture, with new types of labor, methods of accumulation, and formation of class subjects. As Antonio Negri describes it, the new post-Fordist worker is

> ...increasingly directly involved in computer-related, communicative and formative work... shot through and constituted by the continuous interweaving of technoscientific activity and the hard work of production of commodities, by the territoriality of the networks within which this interweaving is distributed, by the increasingly intimate combination of the recomposition of times of labour and of forms of life. (Quoted in Dyer-Witheford 488)

This "immaterial labor," according to Maurizio Lazzarato, is "the cultural and informational content of commodities" whose production requires "cybernetics and computer control." According to Hardt and Negri, immaterial labor "has become hegemonic in qualitative terms and has imposed a tendency on other forms of labour and society itself." While still undertaken by a minority of the global workforce, "today labour and society have to informationalize, become intelligent, become communicative, become affective" (*Multitude* 109). This has led some to declare a new period of capitalist accumulation, called "cognitive capitalism." Yann Moulier Boutang distinguishes cognitive capitalism from merely the valorization of information, which, as he notes, occurred under industrial capitalism, but as the valorization of innovation. Innovation – the production of new concepts, ideas, and business models – cannot, by its very nature, be rationalized. This means that cognitive workers must retain a degree of autonomy in order to produce effectively. "In order to be productive, cognitive capitalism is condemned to live with new and unprecedented degrees of freedom" (41).

Other analysts have noted the challenges inherent in a capitalist economy reliant both on intellectual property and on innovation. Bob Jessop argues that scientific production, even under capitalism, cannot proceed without the kind of collaboration that contravenes intellectual property. "Knowledge is a collectively generated resource and, even where specific forms and types of intellectual property are produced in capitalist conditions for profit, this depends on a far wider intellectual commons" ("The State and the Contradictions of the Knowledge-Driven Economy" 129). Reynolds and Szerszynski, in a Marxian formulation of Boyle's Second Enclosure Movement, identify a "secondary primitive accumulation," by which the existing state-managed scientific commons is "privatized, reorganized, and cannibalized" to satisfy the needs for technological progress under late capitalism.[1]

Carlo Vercellone elaborates on this observation through Marxist categories. In post-Fordist relations of production,

> direct command over the process of production tends to be substituted by command over markets, and this occurs both through the constitution of monopolies and capital's ability to found the appropriation of generated value outside of the company borders by imposing itself as an intermediary between labour and markets in the pursuit of a logic that is reminiscent of that of the putting-out-system.

Rather than control the production process, capital controls markets, allowing workers to manage themselves while appropriating the results, an approach that Vercellone argues "is reminiscent of pre-industrial capitalism and of the formal subsumption of labour under capital" ("The new articulation of wages, rent and profit in cognitive capitalism").

Vercellone's discussion of subsumption refers to the unpublished "sixth chapter" of *Capital* (included in the Penguin edition as "Results of the Immediate Production Process"), a passage to which many autonomist Marxists refer. Marx makes a distinction between two ways that production of value can be organized under capitalism:

> ...if we consider the two forms of surplus-value, absolute and relative, separately, we shall see that absolute surplus-value always precedes relative. To these two forms of surplus-value there correspond two separate forms of the subsumption of labour under capital, or two distinct forms of capitalist production. And here too one form always precedes the other, although the second form, the more highly developed one, can provide the foundations for the introduction of the first in new branches of industry. (*Capital* Vol. 1 1025)

In the first form, formal subsumption "is only formally distinct from earlier modes of production... either when the producer is self-employing or when the immediate producers are forced to deliver surplus labor for others" (ibid). In formal subsumption, the relationship to a capitalist extracting surplus value marks the difference from pre-capitalist craft, but "[t]echnologically speaking, the labour process goes on as before, with the proviso that it is now subordinated to capital" (1026). Under real subsumption, capital restructures the labor process itself by introducing machines: "a complete revolution takes place in the mode of production itself, in the productivity of the workers and in the relations between workers and capitalists" (1035). Formal subsumption corresponds to absolute surplus value, extracted by lengthening the working day; real subsumption produces relative surplus value, by intensifying the productive process.

While it is tempting to read a historical progression from formal subsumption to real subsumption, a careful examination reveals that Marx believed that formal and real subsumption could exist alongside one another: formal subsumption "is a particular form alongside the developed mode of production which is specifically capitalist" (1019). As Patrick Murray describes it,

> the terms 'formal subsumption' and 'real subsumption' refer first to concepts of subsumption and only secondarily – if at all – to historical stages of subsumption. Marx considers the possibility of a distinct historical stage of merely formal subsumption but finds no evidence of one. (252)

In this way, immaterial laborers, such as open-source programmers, labor in formally subsumed relations. Commentators, such as Jessop and Vercellone, suggest that these relations are more beneficial to post-Fordist capitalism as sources of innovation and creativity. But the history of free software demonstrates that formal subsumption is not simply an arrangement with a functional value for capitalism, but the result of a significant struggle: in this sense, formally subsumed work is the fruit of a partial victory, a realization of certain kinds of autonomy, even though it falls short of breaking with capitalism. Rather than a functionalist requirement for capitalist innovation and scientific development, the presence of formal subsumption, rather than real subsumption, in digital spaces is a hard-won outcome of the struggles of hackers, pirates, digital artists, and programmers. The computer underground's manifold initiatives impeded attempts to rationalize digital environments via intellectual property. In their organized efforts to retain control over their labor processes and the use of their digital creations, it furnished productive relations based on the ownership of one's own equipment and the self-management of production, carving out a formally subsumed niche which, for all its contradictions, has allowed a large degree of autonomy.

For Paolo Virno, this autonomy reveals potentials in the working class that Marx did not foresee. "Marx completely identified the general intellect with fixed capital," and thus ignored "the instance when that same general intellect manifests itself on the contrary as *living labor*" (270, italics in original). This living labor represents a "mass intellectuality": "the repository of the indivisible knowledges of living subjects and their linguistic cooperation" (ibid), which is a quality of "the whole social labor force in the post-Fordist era" (271). The development of information technology and the accompanying spread of education have led to a more diffuse and independent working class appropriate for the computer age, one that, rather than producing value within a tightly organized production process, appears to produce it autonomously in a process of self-valorization, only to have it captured through capitalist appropriation. This self-valorizing and self-organizing character of immaterial labor implies, for Hardt and Negri, an egalitarian future: "immaterial labor thus seems to provide the potential for a kind of spontaneous and elementary communism" (294).

For the cognitive capitalist school, the salient difference between immaterial labor and physical labor boils down to management of the labor process. The radical potentials of immaterial labor emerge from capital's requirements to withhold direct management over the labor process, while still claiming the property and profits from the innovations produced. But does such a state of affairs lead, as Negri and

Virno contend, to a new kind of capitalism accompanied by a new kind of revolutionary class of workers?

There are several problems with such a claim. First, much of the autonomist analysis of the potentials of living labor and the organization of capitalism in the form of the "general intellect" relies upon Marx's *Grundrisse*, his preparatory notebooks for writing *Capital*. Marx refined the highly ambiguous and suggestive account of general intellect into the extraction of relative surplus value by machines under the real subsumption of the labor process (Heinrich 95–112; see also Pitts). This trajectory seems to undermine the autonomist critique of the general intellect: Marx refined his concepts to highlight, not the potential for mass intellectuality, but rather the way in which the worker becomes an "appendage of the machine." What Virno sees as mass intellectuality, Marx describes as technologically deskilled labor that is increasingly socialized through advanced technology.

Second, the idea that intellectual labor must be allowed autonomy from managerial and technical control is by no means clear. As George Caffentzis demonstrates, Alan Turing's work on computation reveals that mental labor – the skilled, creative, and innovative work of the immaterial laborers – can also be automated: "if any rule-governed activity is computable, then all repeatable and standardized labour (whether mental or physical) producing commodities is mechanizable" (175). These theoretical points are echoed by a recent spate of speculation about the coming automation of knowledge worker jobs by algorithms and artificial intelligence (for example, Steiner).

Third, the category of immaterial labor is itself in question. Many post-autonomist theorists, confronting a capitalism that is increasingly financialized and reliant on value capture rather than surplus value production, have concluded that Marx's discussion of the labor theory of value no longer applies to the contemporary condition. For Virno, writing in *Grammar of the Multitude*, the general intellect reveals that "so-called 'law of value' (according to which the value of a product is determined by the amount of labor time that went into it), which Marx considers the keystone of modern social relations, is, however, shattered and refuted by capitalist development itself" (100). Similar statements have been made by Hardt and Negri and Vercellone (see Fuchs, "With or Without Marx?" 635). Because of the immateriality of the products produced, and the reliance on cultural, linguistic, and creative competencies, autonomous labor processes can't simply be measured according to labor time.

However, this rests on a misunderstanding of Marx's value theory. The "immateriality" of value was recognized by Marx himself in the very first chapter of *Capital* as the contradiction between use value of the commodity and its exchange value:

> The objectivity of commodities as values differs from Dame Quickly in the sense that "a man knows not where to have it." Not an atom of matter enters into the objectivity of commodities as values; in this sense it is the direct opposite of the coarsely sensuous objectivity of commodities as physical objects. We may twist and turn a single commodity as we wish; it remains impossible to grasp it as a thing possessing value. However, let us remember that commodities possess an objective character as values only in so far as they are all expressions of an identical social substance, human labour, that their objective character as values is therefore purely social. From this it follows self-evidently that it can only appear in the social relation between commodity and commodity. (138–9)

Value, in Marx's theory, refers to a social relationship of exploitation that can only be expressed in relations of commodity to commodity. The measurability, or lack thereof, of value in terms of labor time does not refute Marx's theory: it is, indeed, part of Marx's point.

The subsequent implication that immaterial laborers are the hegemonic workforce in contemporary capitalism contains further problems. As Nick Dyer-Witheford demonstrates in *Cyber-Proletariat*, immaterial digital labor relies upon many forms of labor that more closely resembles the factories and mines of the 19th century, from the toxic manufacture of components to the "artisanal" mining of rare earth minerals for chips. As in Lessig's distinctions between creatives and pirates, the autonomist cognitariat becomes a privileged subject, this time of overcoming capitalism. Meanwhile, the proletariat, located largely in the industrial zones of the Global South, recede from the view of radical theory.

Digital Labor: The Return of Value Theory

More recent Marxist theories of labor and digital technology have returned to Marx's value theory to understand the organization of commercial Internet platforms and social media in more detailed and rigorous way, bereft of optimism of both Free Culture and autonomist theorists. Marx describes the extraction of surplus value in the following way. Commodities acquire value beyond that of their constituent materials because of the special commodity, labor-power, contributed by the worker during the production process. In order to turn a profit, the capitalist must pay the worker a wage that is less than the value of the labor-power contributed to the commodity. Marx discusses this surplus value less in terms of underpayment than in terms of the extension of working time. In order to earn a day's wage, the worker had to labor beyond what was socially necessary to reproduce her labor-power. Such exploitation is a constitutive feature of capitalism.

The audience reception studies of Dallas Smythe were an early and influential application value theory to ad-supported capitalist media. Smythe argued that the relevant commodity in commercial television was not the content, the shows themselves, as viewers did not pay to watch them but consumed them for free. Rather, television functioned to produce the audience-commodity, which was then sold to advertisers. In this formulation, spectatorship becomes a kind of labor performed by audiences in order to produce this commodity. Like labor, viewing time is extended beyond what is socially necessary via advertising.

Digital labor theorists follow Smythe's line of argument: the free services and open navigation provided by Internet corporations function in a similar way as the "free" viewing of television. In reality, most of the digital economy is based on advertising, and so viewing websites and feeds is, following Smythe, the labor which produces the users as a commodity (Fuchs, "Dallas Smythe Today").

In many ways, digital environments make Smythe's ideas of audience labor even more apparent. Web entrepreneur Tim O'Reilly used the term "architectures of participation" to describe Web 2.0's interactive spaces, positing that user activity within commercial platforms would be at the center of the postcrash digital economy. "Participation" then became a keyword for analysts of digital media, from Clay Shirky's enthusiasm for the "cognitive surplus" expended on LOLcats and Wikipedia to Henry Jenkins's extolling of the democratic potentials of new "participatory media" in which fans could take part in media creation. But underpinning the new creative potentials of audiences is an array of data tracking and monitoring. Unlike television audiences, web users are individuated, and each click or mouse movement can become a data point for market research or the means by which to further reshape web infrastructure to better capture audience activity.

For digital labor theorists, these architectures of participation are, in fact, "digital enclosures" subject to heavy surveillance and data mining in order to extract as much information about users as possible, which is then sold to advertisers (Andrejevic). They also provide the "attention labor" (Beller) to advertisements crafted on the basis of these data, ultimately the method of realizing profit online pursued by Facebook and Google. Tiziana Terranova has usefully categorized the varieties of value-generating and value-realizing activity in digital environments as "free labor," which encompasses generating data, producing digital objects and maintaining environments without any payment. "Simultaneously voluntarily given and unwaged, enjoyed and exploited, free labor on the Net includes the activity of building Web sites, modifying software packages, reading and participating in mailing lists, and building virtual spaces on MUDs and MOOs" (Terranova 33).

In this way, the navigation of digital environments, and the use of digital tools – software, applications, games – are themselves productive. Users produce data, which companies then use to modify their products and tailor advertising campaigns. Elements of cultural production, such as photo editing or music production, are automated, deskilled, and enclosed inside proprietary environments. This deskilling allows consumers to take part in the production process, becoming the "prosumers" of Alvin Toffler's predictions, or the "mass customizers" beloved of management theory (Gilmore and Pine). This dramatic reshaping of labor processes for cultural work drives the deprofessionalization and informalization of this work into amateur labor, volunteer labor, and involuntary forms of surplus value extraction. Audiences no longer merely produce themselves as a commodity to be sold to a third party; they are increasingly a component of the media production process itself. As Christian Fuchs puts it, "prosumption is used for outsourcing work to users and consumers, who work without payment. Thereby corporations reduce their investment- and labour-costs, jobs are destroyed, and consumers who work for free are extremely exploited" ("Dallas Smythe Today" 711).

Digital labor theory is an elegant reframing of liberal theories of the digital economy. "Participation" as used by Web 2.0 enthusiasts such as O'Reilly, Shirky, and Jenkins is actually the form labor takes in networks. Users of Internet services are in fact laborers, who do not recognize themselves as such, and therefore rarely question the system of ownership and value production erected by Internet companies. The saturation of digital networks with value-producing activity is not, as Hardt and Negri argue, the final dispensation of the labor theory of value, but actually its extension. Even when engaged in voluntary projects utilizing their skills in their free time, users are still subject to capitalism's commodifying logic.

While the free labor thesis has the sheen of a Copernican revolution, irrevocably altering the understanding of the digital economy afterwards, it too contains limits. Because so much rests upon advertising rates generated by reliable audiences, free labor business models are tenuous and unstable: it is not enough to extract surplus value from users clicking through pages, and such value must be realized on the market. At this conjuncture, most web services are supported, not from advertising revenue, but from venture capital financing. And web companies also hire thousands of waged workers, from privileged high-level programmers to content moderators paid a pittance to remove offensive imagery from networks. Many of these workers are exploited in a less novel sense than what Fuchs has problematically referred to as the "infinitely exploited" productive users of Facebook ("Labor in Informational Capitalism and on the Internet" 191): they are subject to the "old" labor theory of value, by which they toil beyond the value of their wages in order to secure profit for owners. Nevertheless, the free labor thesis opens up an understanding of how capitalism profits from the formally subsumed, informal organizations of the Internet.

The next chapter will examine the historical development of online media piracy in light of the preceding description of digital labor movements, as well as the influential ideologies that become a part of the movement's complex and contradictory self-understanding. It will think through piracy not as merely political activity, but as activity politicized through its interaction with work and its valorization.

Note

1 This is a common conflation of two distinct historical forms of property: *res communes* (common things without ownership) and *res publicae* (things owned and administered by the state). See Berry, 79–97.

Works Cited

Andrejevic, Mark. "Surveillance in the Digital Enclosure." *The Communication Review* 10.4 (2007): 295–317.

Barbrook, Richard and Andy Cameron. "The Californian Ideology." *Science as Culture* 6.1 (1996): 44–72.

Beller, Jonathan. *The Cinematic Mode of Production: Attention Economy and Society of the Spectacle.* Hanover, NH: Dartmouth College P, 2006.

Benkler, Yochai. *The Wealth of Networks.* New Haven, CT: Yale UP, 2006.

Berry, David. *Copy, Rip, Burn: the Politics of Copyleft and Open Source.* London: Pluto P, 2008.

Bollier, David. *Viral Spiral: How the Commoners Built a Digital Republic of Their Own.* New York, NY: The New P, 2008.

Bourriard, Nicolas. *Post-production.* Trans. Jeanine Herman. New York, NY: Lukas & Sternberg, 2002.

Boutang, Yann-Moulier. *Cognitive Capitalism.* Trans. Ed Emery. Cambridge: Polity, 2012.

Boyle, James. *Public Domain: Enclosing the Commons of the Mind.* New Haven, CT: Yale UP, 2008.

———. "The Second Enclosure Movement and the Construction of the Public Domain." *Law and Contemporary Problems* 66.33 (2003): 33–52.Caffentzis, George. *In Letters of Blood and Fire: Work, Machines, and the Crisis of Capitalism.* Oakland, CA: PM P, 2013.

Castoriadis, Cornelius. *Political and Social Writings, Volume 2.* Trans. David Ames Curtis. Minneapolis: U of Minnesota P, 1988.

Coleman, Gabriella. "Code is Speech: Liberalism, Legality, and the Ethics of Free Software." *Cultural Anthropology* 24.3 (2009): 420–454.

Coleman, E. Gabriella and Alex Golub. "Hacker Practice: Moral Genres and the Cultural Articulation of Liberalism." *Anthropological Theory* 8.3 (Sept. 2008): 255–277.

Coleman, Biella and Mako Hill. "How Free Became Open and Everything Else Under the Sun." *M/C Journal: A Journal of Media and Culture* 7.3 (2004): n. pag.

Coombe, Rosemary. *The Cultural Life of Intellectual Property: Authorship, Appropriation, and the Law.* Durham, NC: Duke UP, 1998.

Dafermos, George and Johan Söderberg. "The Hacker Movement as a Continuation of Labour Struggle." *Capital & Class* 97 (2009): 53–73.

Dalla Costa, Maria and Selma James. *The Power of Women and the Subversion of the Community.* 3rd ed. London: Falling Wall P, 1973.

de Certeau, Michel. *The Practice of Everyday Life.* Trans. Steven Rendall. Berkeley: U of California P, 1988.

Deleuze, Gilles. "Postscript on the Societies of Control." *October* 59 (1992): 3–7.

Dyer-Witheford, Nick. *Cyber-Proletariat: Global Labour in the Digital Vortex.* London: Pluto P, 2015.

Federici, Sylvia. "Wages against Housework." *Revolution at Point Zero.* Oakland, CA: PM P, 2012. 15–22.

Florida, Richard. *The Rise of the Creative Class.* New York, NY: Perseus Book Group, 2002.

Foucault, Michel. "What Is an Author?" *Aesthetics, Method, and Epistemology.* Ed. James D. Faubion. Trans. Robert Hurley et al. New York, NY: The New P, 1998. 205–222.

Fuchs, Christian. "Dallas Smythe Today – The Audience Commodity, the Digital Labour Debate, Marxist Political Economy and Critical Theory." *tripleC: Communication, Capitalism & Critique* 10.2 (2012) 692–740. Web. 22 Apr. 2015.

———. "Labor in Informational Capitalism and on the Internet." *The Information Society* 26.3 (2010): 179–196. Web. 22 Apr. 2015.

———. "With or Without Marx? With or Without Capitalism? A Rejoinder to Adam Arvidsson and Eleanor Colleoni." *tripleC: Communication, Capitalism & Critique* 10.2 (2012): 633–645. Web. 22 Apr. 2015.

Gilmore, James H. and B. Joseph Pine II. *Markets of One: Creating Customer-Unique Value through Mass Communication.* Cambridge, MA: Harvard Business School P, 2000.

Hardt, Michael. "Jefferson and Democracy." *American Quarterly* 59.1 (Mar. 2007): 41–78. Web. 23 Apr. 2015.

Hardt, Michael and Antonio Negri. *Multitude: War and Democracy in the Age of Empire.* New York, NY: Penguin, 2004.

Heinrich, Michael. "The 'Fragment on Machines': A Marxian Misconception in the Grundrisse and its Overcoming in *Capital.*" *In Marx's Laboratory: Critical Interpretations of the Grundrisse.* Eds. Riccardo Bellofiore, Guido Starosta, and Peter D. Thomas. Leiden: Brill, 2015. 197–212.

Howkins, John. *The Creative Economy: How People Make Money from Ideas.* London: Penguin, 2013.

Jenkins, Henry. *Convergence Culture: Where Old and New Media Collide.* New York, NY: New York UP, 2006.

Jessop, Bob. "The State and the Contradictions of the Knowledge-driven Economy." *Knowledge, Space, Economy.* Eds. John Bryson, Peter Daniels, Nick Henry, and Jane Pollard. London: Routledge, 2000.

Kelty, Chris. *Two Bits: The Cultural Significance of Free Software.* Durham, NC: Duke UP, 2008.

Kleiner, Dmytri. *The Telekommunist Manifesto.* Amsterdam: Colophon, 2010. Web. 12 June 2014.

Lazzarato, Mauricio. "Immaterial Labour." Trans. Paul Colilli and Ed. Emery. *Generation Online,* n.d. Web. 19 April 2012.

Lessig, Lawrence. *Free Culture: The Nature and Future of Creativity.* New York, NY: Penguin Books, 2004.

Linebaugh, Peter and Marcus Rediker. *The Many-Headed Hydra: Sailors, Slaves, Commoners, and the Hidden History of the Revolutionary Atlantic.* Boston, MA: Beacon P, 2005.

Losurdo, Domenico. *Liberalism: A Counter-History.* Trans. Gregory Elliott. London: Verso, 2011.

Marx, Karl. *Capital: A Critique of Political Economy, Volume 1.* Trans. Ben Fowkes. London: Penguin Books, 1992.

———. *A Contribution to the Critique of Political Economy.* Translated by N.I. Stone. Chicago, IL: Charles H. Kerr and Co, 1911.

———. *Grundrisse: Foundations of the Critique of Political Economy.* Trans. Martin Nicolaus. London: Penguin Books, 1993.

McLeod, Kembrew. *Freedom of Expression: Overzealous Copyright Bozos and Other Enemies of Creativity.* New York, NY: Doubleday, 2005.

Murray, Patrick. "The Social and Material Transformation of Production by Capital: Formal and Real Subsumption in Capital, Volume I." *The Constitution of Capital.* Eds. Riccardo Bellofiore and Nicola Taylor. Basingstoke: Palgrave Macmillan, 2004. 243–273.

O'Reilly, Tim. "The Architecture of Participation." *O'Reilly.* June 2004. Web. 12 June 2014.

Pashukanis, Evgenii. *The General Theory of Law and Marxism*. Trans. Barbara Einhorn. New Brunswick, NJ: Transaction Publishers, 2003.

Pitts, Frederick Harry. *Critiquing Capitalism Today: New Ways to Read Marx*. Basingstoke: Palgrave Macmillan, 2018.

Philip, Kavita. "What Is a Technological Author? The Pirate Function and Intellectual Property." *Postcolonial Studies* 8.2 (2005): 199–218.

Raymond, Eric. "The Cathedral and the Bazaar." *The Cathedral and the Bazaar*. 18 Feb. 2010. Web. 13 Dec. 2015.

Rediker, Marcus. *Villains of All Nations: Atlantic Pirates in the Golden Age*. Boston, MA: Beacon P, 2005.

Reynolds, Laurence and Bronislaw Szerszynski. "Neoliberalism and Technology: Perpetual Innovation or Perpetual Crisis?" *Neoliberalism and Technoscience: Critical Approaches*. Eds. Luigi Pellizzoni and Marja Ylönen. Farnham: Ashgate, 2012. 27–46.

Shirky, Clay. *Cognitive Surplus: How Technology Makes Consumers into Collaborators*. New York, NY: Penguin, 2011.

Smith, Tony. "A Critical Assessment of *The Wealth of Networks*." *Taking Socialism Seriously*. Eds. Anatole Anton and Richard Schmitt. London: Lexington Books, 2012. 155–184.

Stallman, Richard. *Free Software, Free Society: Selected Essays of Richard M. Stallman*. Ed. Joshua Gay. Scotts Valley, CA: CreateSpace, 2009. Web. 15 Nov. 2012.

Steiner, Christopher. *Automate This: How Algorithms Came to Rule Our World*. New York, NY: Penguin, 2012.

Terranova, Tiziana. "Free Labor: Producing Culture for the Digital Economy." *Social Text* 18.2 63 (Summer 2000): 33–58.

Thomas, Douglas. *Hacker Culture*. Minneapolis: U of Minnesota P, 2003.

Thompson, E.P. *The Making of the English Working Class*. New York, NY: Vintage, 1966.

Toffler, Alvin. *The Third Wave*. New York, NY: Bantam Books, 1980.

Vercellone, Carlo. "The New Articulation of Wages, Rent and Profit in Cognitive Capitalism." *The Art of Rent*. Feb. 2008, Queen Mary University School of Business and Management, London.

Virno, Paolo. *A Grammar of the Multitude: For an Analysis of Contemporary Forms of Life*. Trans. Isabella Bertoletti, James Cacaito, and Andrea Casson. Los Angeles, CA: Semiotext(e), 2004.

———. "Notes on the 'General Intellect.'" *Marxism beyond Marxism*. Eds. Saree Makdisi, Cesare Casarino, and Rebecca E. Karl. New York, NY/ London: Routledge, 1996. 265–272.

Wark, McKenzie. *A Hacker Manifesto*. Cambridge, MA: Harvard UP, 2004.

Woodmansee, Martha. "The Genius and Copyright: Economic and Legal Conditions of the Emergence of the 'Author.'" *Eighteenth-Century Studies* 17.4 (1984): 425–448.

3   A History of Digital Piracy

As discussed previously, free software hackers waged the first battles over intellectual property on computer networks. Their struggles centered on preserving autonomous labor practices in the face of a quickly commodifying and rationalizing economy of software development, which sought docile consumers, not independent petty producers. The development of "open source" software and the Web 2.0 economy of digital labor cooled some of these tensions, but it did not eradicate them. Intellectual property remains a tool that media producers use to attempt to control both production and consumption on digital networks, channeling these activities into rationalized, predictable avenues.

The resistance to such rationalization and commodification among other early users of computer networks often understood the struggle as the free software movement did: as one over skill and autonomy over productive and consumptive activity. These were the earliest digital pirates, a classification given to them by the software industry, but one that many soon adopted with pride.

Some of the earliest discourse produced by these pirates voiced a concern over skill-based autonomy. Piratical practices, such as copying and exchanging software for free, were central to the first wave of personal computing enthusiasts. To stop these practices, commercial software companies began to insert copy protections on their software, which prevented users from copying and sharing purchases. As is often the case, these copy protections produced side effects that further restricted the behavior of software purchasers. Chiefly, consumers could not make backups, which were especially important for those tinkering with code: it gave them the ability to revert back to original code, and the ability to distribute copies of software to others in the interest of collective learning and work.

Such technologically encoded copy protections have raised many objections. In *Code and Other Laws of Cyberspace*, Lawrence Lessig warns that coded mechanisms of control take power away from the judicial system, which works for the public good, and favor absolutist control at the hands of content owners, enacting a disturbing lack of democratic oversight. Tarleton Gillespie sounds a similar note in *Wired Shut*. Such copy protections are a perfect example of the control mechanisms described by Deleuze: they regulate access to information and by doing so replace the function of declining social institutions.

Before academics began writing about them, software copy protections sparked enormous turmoil among early personal computer enthusiasts. To restore the ability to copy, small software companies began to release programs capable of breaking copy protection, such as Locksmith for the Apple II. In response, software magazines, the chief organ for promoting software, blacklisted these companies at the behest of their larger advertisers. These actions were anathema to hacker values of free expression and unrestricted computer usage. The controversy provoked hobbyist Charles Haight to start his own magazine. The first issue of *Hardcore Computing*, from 1981, begins with an editorial written by Haight's brother Bev, excoriating the complicity of magazine publishers with the software industry: "They don't want their readers to back up 'protected' disks! CENSORSHIP in computer magazines" (4–5). Haight lambasts software magazines for quietly refusing to run Locksmith ads as censorship: "They are obviously withholding information in an attempt to mislead their readership" (5).

Haight positions emerging practices of skill development against regressive anti-piracy initiatives. Copyright is an "outdated, obsolete system" and "is one of the obstacles that stand in the way of the technological evolution of information exchange (hereafter called info-x)" (5). The preservation of existing piratical practices is an essential element of developing newly necessary skills, themselves a cornerstone of freedom in the age of "info-x." In this, Haight articulates a moral-technical order akin to the one Chris Kelty identifies in free software developers, one directly antagonistic to commercial software. The use value of software is reconceived as a pedagogical tool: by tinkering with code, users, productively consuming software, will themselves learn to program. However, software companies have rhetorically delegitimated these practices:

> When the editors speak of "pirates," they are referring to you and me and our "innocent," casual exchanges of software. We are the pirates! We are that "threat to the entire software market." It

would not be too erroneous to say that we, the software consumers, are all pirates!... Something is terribly wrong with any system that labels all its consumers as "criminals" and pirates of the most vile kind. (ibid)

In an act of militant resistance, *Hardcore Computing* not only ran ads for software such as Locksmith, but also published instructions for how programmers themselves could defeat copy protection by tinkering with source code. These would later become a standard kind of article among software pirates: the cracking tutorial. *Hardcore Computing*, with its irreverence to intellectual property and emphasis on subversive skill promotion, presaged the pirate zines of the early software piracy counterculture.

Bulletin Board Systems and Warez

As Johann Söderberg has pointed out, the people deeply involved in digital piracy are often involved in other aspects of the hacker underground. This was especially true of early digital piracy on Bulletin Board Systems (BBS), an early way to connect computers via telephone lines. A BBS is not a network in the same sense as the Internet as we know it today, but was organized on telephone lines. Rather than a web of interconnection, users connected their computers by "calling" each other on telephone lines, thus limiting the number of simultaneous connections, and, if connecting to a BBS outside one's area code, accruing long-distance charges. Rather than the open web, a BBS is a smaller, more exclusive method of connecting, and individual BBS hosts tailored their boards to specific interests, often connected to exploring the capabilities of computing and telephony.

In the 1980s, personal computers were a rarity, and modems even rarer, cultivating feelings of exclusivity, of being part of a hidden world where one could assume a different identity. As Douglas Thomas documents in his study of early hacker culture, BBSs had a particular attraction to young people, particularly adolescent males, who found a space where they could challenge conventions of parental and societal authority in safe environs, while also demonstrating technical mastery. And indeed, these were often heavily male spaces. According to Jordan and Taylor's taxonomy of hacker culture, one recurring component is "male dominance and an associated misogyny" and "a macho, competitive attitude" (767). This carried over to the software pirate scene, which was heavily, if not exclusively, male.

Imbued with the values of teenage rebellion, the BBS computer underground coalesced around the cachet attached to boasting about disruptive computer practices. These practices were grouped together under the label HPAV: hacking (testing and breaking into systems), phreaking (acquiring free telephone time), anarchy (committing petty crime and vandalism), and viruses (malicious programs). Piracy too became an integral part of the BBS computer underground. The hacker practice of transgressive displays of skill found a powerful outlet in the "cracking" of software protections and the distribution of pirated versions of software and games. The earliest pirates reveled in their rebel identity, much like the Haights, taking pseudonyms that highlighted their illegal activity: individual pirates like the Apple Bandit, the Burglar, Black Bart, Copy/Cat, and Rogue Pirate; and groups like Midwest Pirates Guild, West Coast Pirate Exchange, Racketeers, and Hi-Rez Hijackers.

Initially a way to distribute, test, and learn software, piracy took on a new cast in the BBS underground: it became a competitive quest for status among different bulletin boards, with technical skill as the ultimate status marker. System operators (sysops) of a BBS had control over who could access the board, and therefore, any files hosted there. Having exclusive files, and having them before anyone else, became a way to mark one's bulletin board as part of the elite: those who possess autonomy in digital environments. Décary-Hetu et al. argue that the entire social organization of the software piracy scene rests on status recognition, though Hargadon amends "the ability to translate this into more favourable access on coveted systems" (136) to the motivations of pirates. In control societies, access is a highly sought ability, and even a source of social status.

Unauthorized copies of software were abbreviated as "warez," a kind of pirate commodity with its own production and distribution system, and its own peculiar methods of consumption. Competitive pressures for status among pirate crews led to a coherent organizational form among BBS pirates, who organized into small flexible, fluctuating crews, though with remarkably standardized divisions of labor. Most crews lasted less than a year, and members constantly circulated. In many ways, they were exemplary of post-Fordist management structures: loose confederations of individuals who come together for short-term projects, often rotate jobs, and are led based on personal qualities, such as charisma and skill, rather than formalized hierarchy.

Technologically determinist perspectives on digital piracy, which posit that it is an inevitable side effect of the inadequacies of copyright in the age of digital networks, tend to ignore its organizational element, along with the meanings and values which adhere to it: what we might call, for the sake of brevity, the culture of digital piracy.

The totality of pirate organizations, termed "The Scene," derives its form from the BBS era of computer networking. Many practices are holdovers from the days of BBS pirates, and even today The Scene is still the ultimate origin for the majority of pirated releases of content on peer-to-peer (P2P) networks (Howe). Within The Scene, groups of pirates race to be the first to secure and release pirated versions of digital content, a remainder from the days when BBS boards competed for status and members.

Goldman has mapped out the division of labor in the scene:

> These operations divide up several discrete tasks among their members, including sourcing new warez, cracking any technological protection devices, testing the cracked warez to make sure they still work, packaging the warez for easy distribution, couriering the warez to propagate the warez to other sites or throughout the Internet, performing systems administration on the computers used by the group, and managing/overseeing the operations. (396)

The first role is that of the supplier, who must acquire the original content to be pirated. In the early days of BBS, this simply meant purchasing a program from the store. A BBS could rely on a well-heeled member to do this, but some boards also engaged in credit card fraud to purchase both the hardware required to run a board as well as the programs to distribute on it. Eventually, top pirate organizations established moles inside companies, who provided them with advanced access to content. Goldman cites cases in which employees of Intel and Microsoft were prosecuted for cooperating with pirate groups. Advance review copies are another frequent source, as illustrated in the case of *Doom II*, which emerged on pirate networks weeks before its official release date (Kline, Dyer-Witheford, and de Peuter), indicating an internal leak. More recently, a rip of *The Secret Life of Walter Mitty* appeared on pirate networks containing watermark indicating the original source as a screener copy belonging to Ellen Degeneres (Spangler). These examples illustrate that piracy is a component of resistance to normal functioning of business occurring outside of digital networks. Pirates are, for the most part, wage laborers, many in the information technology and media industries, and some for the very companies their piratical practices undermine. The Scene is an insurgent sector of IT labor, which transforms mundane work into games of status and ability.

The second, and arguably the most important, role in a pirate organization is the cracker, who must circumvent copy protections on programs in order to make them available to any user and thus an effective pirate commodity. Often this is done through tinkering with the source code of the program, a task requiring a high level of coding ability. Because of this, cracking presents a prime opportunity for programmers to transgressively display their coding skills to their peers. Crackers were the initial overlap between hackers and pirates in the BBS scene.

Crackers are also one of the most productive roles in a pirate network. They alter code just as a professional software developer might, oftentimes improving the program. Wasiak describes the correction of source code by video game crackers: "the removal of all noticed errors and glitches in the original code, since the cracked game was meant to be superior to the original in every possible way" (8). As Reunanen has put it, "the cracker system can be seen as an offspring and a mirror image of the commercial model."

The skill in programming required for cracking have made crackers a cherished part of the computer underground. Cracking is a way for participants to train themselves in programming skill, a major value of the computer underground. As Pirate Magazine, one of the many online zines distributed through the BBS underground, put it, "Cracking is about learning computer programming, and the fun is in increasing skills." It is "one of the best (and most fun) ways to learn about what makes a program work" ("Cracking Tips (Part 1)").

Once cracked, programs were transferred by couriers to other BBSS as a sort of trophy, and a way to establish affiliations ("affilz") among other pirate boards: a way of rewarding good work with expanded access. A low-skill role, couriers are often newer members in pirate organizations.

As the division of labor sedimented and the warez scene grew, pirated goods became more sophisticated, and incorporated a greater variety of labor. Pirates began inserting their own introductory animations and musical compositions into cracked programs. These "cracktros" served to brand releases and show off the programming and compositional skills of pirates.[1] Crews put together "releases" (files compressed into a single .ZIP file) which reduced the file size while including an .NFO file containing information about the crew who created it as well as multicolored artwork, known as ANSI art (referring to the text and color outputs established by the American National Standards Institute). Through these releases they mimicked, often in an irreverent way, commercially available products. Pirate releases operate as a performative critique of the capitalist flow of digital commodities, a way to creatively articulate the vision for an alternatively organized digital space.

This alternative organization was not an alternative to capitalism. Software pirates did not attempt to create an anti-capitalist space, but rather a differently organized capitalist space, with a more autonomous relationship to commodification and consumption. While members of the BBS underground dabbled in credit card fraud (often to purchase software and hardware to keep the scene running), pirated software was understood as explicitly noncommercial (Goldman). An early BBS scene magazine spells this out explicitly:

> What's a pirate? COMPUTER PIRACY is copying and distribution of copyright software (warez). Pirates are hobbyists who enjoy collecting and playing with the latest programs. Most pirates enjoy collective warez, getting them running, and then generally archive them, or store them away. A PIRATE IS NOT A BOOTLEGGER. Bootleggers are to piracy what a chop-shop is to a home auto mechanic.[2] Bootleggers are people who DEAL stolen merchandise for personal gain. ("So You Want to Be a Pirate?")

Indeed, as pirates themselves have repeatedly avowed, pirates dutifully purchase goods. Thomas and Meyer, sociologists who experimented with publishing their research in the format of a pirate zine text file, argued, "software pirates... report spending considerably more money purchasing software than the average user. Many of these purchases are for trading, and there is a strong ethos in the pirate world that if one uses a program, one purchases it." Subsequent research indicates that pirates tend to purchase more media goods than those who do not pirate (Karaganis). Software pirates also argued that their practices spread computer literacy among young people who were unable to purchase software, but would become good consumers later in life. The .NFO files in pirate releases, which served as a kind of manifesto or newsletter for release groups, often contained exhortations to support quality software releases: "IF YOU ENJOYED THIS PRODUCT, BUY IT! SOFTWARE AUTHORS DESERVE SUPPORT!!" (Smith).

In this way, piracy does not reject commodification outright. Rather, pirates seek to manage the deluge of expensive software in an economically viable way, testing products and developing skills before deciding what to buy. This bears strong similarities to the strategy of autoreduction in 1970s Italy, during which workers resisted inflation and price increases on goods and services by simply paying the old price. Cherki and Wieviorka identify how these struggles had "stakes tied to consumption" (72): working-class neighborhoods organized, with unions, against rate hikes for utilities and services by refusing to pay the new rates. The battles to lower prices for commodities were taken up by the formal labor movement itself, as struggles extended beyond the workplace.

The software industry responded to the warez Scene with legal repression. The No Electronic Theft (NET) Act of 1997 closed the loophole that permitted noncommercial file sharing, redefining financial gain as receipt, or "expectation of receipt, of anything of value, including the receipt of other copyrighted works" (Heneghan 27). This criminalized the bartering and ratio systems, which had regulated exchange in The Scene. Included in the NET Act were stiff penalties, including prison time. The Digital Millennium Copyright Act (DMCA) followed close behind, making the cracking of copy protections illegal, and providing a framework for rights holders to demand the removal of copyrighted content from servers. Social struggles soon cropped up as hackers tested the limits of the DMCA, most fervently around the DeCSS case, where a Norwegian teenager cracked the Content Scramble System (CSS) used on commercial DVDs, enabling users to rip and copy them (Chris Kelty's *Two Bits* extensively documents this case). Subsequent police raids drove dedicated members into more obscure corners of the Internet and, in turn, elevated the barriers to entry into the subculture.

The organizational form developed by BBS warez pirates persists today. Many of the pirated goods trafficked on P2P file-sharing systems such as BitTorrent originate from groups within the old Scene structure, whose creative practices, such as crew names and NFO manifestos, remain intact. In spite of an ever-changing distributional landscape for digital media, much pirated content passes through The Scene's distributional hierarchy, which crystallized in the 1990s. First come exclusive high-level File Transfer Protocol (FTP) sites operated by elite pirate organization. Pirate files then trickle down to less exclusive FTP sites, through Internet Relay Chat (IRC) channels, and eventually to P2P networks, such as BitTorrent, which are disdained by top-level pirates.

MP3, P2P, and the Massification of Piracy

P2P piracy comes out of the audio piracy subculture, which itself emerged from the warez scene, connected through IRC, which replaced BBS as a communicative tool. The history of this subculture is of utmost importance in the development of digital piracy, not the least because it clearly demonstrates the ways in which capital acts to decompose mass opposition and recompose it into new sources of value and profit. Audio piracy is also the point where digital piracy became a mass, rather than niche, phenomenon, thus setting the tone for the struggles to follow.

Music lagged behind software within pirate cultures due to its lack of a file format that possessed a balance of quality and appropriate file size for distribution through the connection speeds and hard drives of the time. This changed with the development of the MP3 format. The MP3 format works by compressing audio algorithmically: a program determines which audio frequencies are unnecessary for the human ear and eliminates them, thus reducing the file size and facilitating transfer over networks.

Yet the invention of the MP3 is, in a sense, a minor component of its flowering into the dominant music format of the first decade of the 21st century. Until its discovery by pirates, it was a series of patents and codecs without a clear use. Even with technological advancements in bandwidth and compression, the record industry had little interest in pursuing online distribution. Alderman documents that "throughout the 1990s, when it came to the Internet, the [record] labels cooperated more than usual. The majors had agreed to drag their heels at every possible step when it came to the Net" (84).

It was pirates who established the MP3 as the preferred file format for digital music in the first decade of the 21st century, and who developed many of its uses. As Jonathan Sterne describes it,

> An Australian hacker acquired L3Enc [the codec owned by German firm Fraunhofer which compressed audio into the MP3 format] using a stolen credit card. The hacker then reverse-engineered the software, wrote a new user interface, and redistributed it for free, naming it 'thank you Fraunhofer.' (201–2)

As a result, MP3s became the preferred file format for digital sound recordings among pirates, and, thus practically everyone else since, at the time, no legitimate digital format for music existed.

Pirate crews devoted to MP3 releases started in 1996. Just as the software pirates, these pirates were creative. They established quality standards for releases (ironically called the "RIAA" in a dig against the record industry lobbying group the Recording Industry Association of America) via an organization called the MP3 Council. Pirates determined which level of audio compression was of suitable fidelity for playback. Pirates also pioneered the use of metadata tags to label individual MP3s as well as the standard file structure for organizing albums ("Recap," "Netfrack"). Some groups released homemade mixes in addition to MP3s of commercial music releases ("Beatforge"). In a time when commercially available MP3s were simply not available, pirates developed many of the practices behind digital music.

Sean Fanning was part of this MP3 warez scene, spending his spare time in an IRC channel called "w00w00" (Menn 19). He sought to automate many of the inconvenient aspects of MP3 exchange and set to work on a program named after his childhood nickname: Napster. Other members of the channel, including future partner Sean Parker, provided free assistance along the model of uncompensated peer production described by Benkler. The program quickly became an enormous success, garnering 32 million users in less than a year, before quickly shutting down in the face of lawsuits from the recording industry.

Behind Napster's rapid success was a structure that, for all its apparent novelty, reproduced elements of the older warez infrastructure. As Merriden describes it, Napster hearkens back to the small, closed networks of the BBS:

> Napster is, in some ways, something of a regression to the old days of the Internet. Mass usage of the Internet has meant that servers have to be used to house information. Napster, on the other hand, relies on communication between the personal computers of the members of the Napster community. (5)

Rather than host MP3 files on its own server, which would be both expensive and highly illegal, Napster acted as a mere listing service, aggregating the names of users and the files they shared into a list that was updated in real time. Data transfer happened between users: from peer to peer. However, as Burk notes, such architecture failed to protect Napster from liability for copyright. The court ruled Napster guilty of secondary and vicarious infringement: "Napster constituted the cyberspace equivalent of a swap meet landowner: it controlled who logged onto and who traded music on its system." As a result, subsequent P2P networks would eschew any centralization as a means to insulate themselves from liability.

Andrea Guzman and Steve Jones document how the business press framed Napster "as a simultaneously ingenious and nefarious technology that was spurring a cultural and economic revolution": a Schumpeterian disrupter with youth culture cachet. The myth of small nimble entrepreneurs facing off against large corporate behemoths remains foundational to Silicon Valley and digital subcultures, but a careful examination of the record reveals very different intentions, actions, and statements from Fanning, as well as the users whose computers built the network. By most accounts, Fanning himself had more interest in technology than in monetizing it; the business side became the priority of his uncle and the partners he brought in. Monetizing Napster presented a significant legal problem: many infractions for piracy hinged on whether the accused profited or not (Menn 102).

The battle over Napster provoked an astonishing amount of activism and political discourse. The program appeared at an important conjuncture, particularly for young people. Napster exploded at the same time that the record industry was settling a class action lawsuit over gouging consumers by fixing the price on CDs (Lieberman). In this light, an exploited and ruthlessly controlled audience discovered the means to refuse to play by the old rules of music production, distribution, and consumption. Napster was also tremendously popular on college campuses, which Gantz and Rochester link to the costs for high education, which had begun to skyrocket (190–2). College students fought attempts to restrict the usage of the program on university networks, and often won (Alderman 112, Menn 135).

The Napster message board became a locus of highly politicized language, which criticized the law, business, and the music industry. "We know it's illegal. We just don't think it's wrong," said one user about downloading music files (Menn 141). Users' rejection of property rights over music did not stop with the record industry, but also extended to artists who sought to shore up copyright. When heavy metal band Metallica filed lawsuits against Napster and its users, it sparked enormous backlash, with one fan proclaiming "Fuck you, Lars. It's our music too!" (144).

Napster's importance lay in how it deskilled the process of piracy, making the practice of sharing music files easy, and close to automatic. Via its networking protocols and simple interface, it provided the technical composition necessary for an already-composed class of consumers. However, this also put it at odds with the existing digital pirate subculture.

Elite pirates and hackers often have a vexed relationship to technology. Because their social status is tied to skill, and because, as Harry Braverman demonstrates, technology is introduced into productive processes in order to deskill work, elite users often resist the imposition of new technologies into their work environments, even as they celebrate technology in other ways. A strong prelapsarian streak runs through the interviews with pirates contained within textfile zines: the Scene is always less enjoyable, too greedy, or too chaotic compared to an earlier iteration.[3]

There is a documented technological drag in digital piracy, in which established practices remain even after they are obsolete, reminiscent of what Raymond Williams refers to as residual cultural formations. In one prominent case of this drag, warez organizations insisted software releases be packaged as a series of 1.44 MB chunks – the size of a 3.5″ floppy disk – even after such disks were obsolete. This practice carried over to MP3s once the file format was accepted by the warez scene ("Netfrack"). Incorporating MP3s into the warez scene was itself a battle: many pirates simply thought ripping a CD was too easy to form the ground for skill display, a belief furiously contested by MP3 enthusiasts who argued that crafting a high-quality MP3 with existing codecs was quite a challenge. Automation plagued the warez MP3 scene as well. Huizing and van der Wal argue that "de-skilling of sceners' tasks [by software and bots] considerably reduced the social interaction on IRC."

However, just as this kind of deskilling of piracy threatened its skill-celebrating traditions, it broadened the struggle against intellectual property by massifying decommodified exchange of MP3s: at least 50 million users at its peak. I want to suggest that Napster revealed a more revolutionary potential than the elite piracy of The Scene. The Scene's politics are centered on maintaining privileges via their skill, which causes them to distance themselves from unskilled users, while they oppose the deskilling effects of the Taylorizing Internet. It is P2P systems, which not only seem to analogize a kind of communism of abundance and noncommodified horizontal exchange for use – P2P rather than client-server, as Dmitri Kleiner puts it in *The Telekommunist Manifesto* – but also have the most radical potentials.

This recalls Walter Benjamin's meditations on the effects of technology on cultural production. A writer who often struggled financially, Benjamin was acutely aware of the divide between left intellectuals and the masses with which they aligned politically: occupying a "position between classes" ("Author as Producer"). However, new technologies of mass production threatened this division: "an increasing number of readers became writers" with the extension of the press. "Thus, the distinction between author and public is about to lose its basic character.... At any moment the reader is ready to turn into a writer" ("The Work of Art in the Age of Mechanical Reproduction"). This loss of distinction would also mean the loss of the writer's profession, but the proletarianization of the writer would mean a greater political charge, as writers would become part of the revolutionary class. However, "even the proletarianization of an intellectual almost never makes a proletarian" ("Author as Producer"): the intellectual's own skills mean that they will always retain some privileges. Total renunciation is impossible; rather, the intellectual must betray their status by changing "from a reproducer of the apparatus of production into an engineer who sees his task as the effort of adapting that apparatus to the aims of the proletarian revolution." This betrayal occurs not at the level of individual commitment and volition, nor by simply taking over the existing means of production, but by transforming the means of production toward more expansive and revolutionary aims. This is precisely what Sean Fanning achieved: he transformed the means of elite piratical circulation into a mass phenomenon which created a situation where the majority of recorded music was exchanged in decommodified ways, and which severed entire swaths of the population from the existing music industry apparatus.

Napster also caused reverberations among those who labored to create music: the artists themselves. While some artists, such as Metallica, lined up with the labels, many artists used the space opened by Napster to criticize the prevailing capitalist organization of music. Prince, who later turned against Internet-distributed music altogether, enthused on his website how Napster revealed the possibility of music released without interference from labels (BBC). The Recording Artists Coalition, an artist group that included stars such as Billy Joel and Sheryl Crow, used the attention to recording industry practices produced from the Napster debates to lobby for reforms of exploitative major label practices (Menn 168). They succeeded having an RIAA-supported clause designating recordings as "works for hire" (which would not qualify for royalty payments) repealed. In 2002, shortly after the Napster boom-and-bust, Courtney Love gave a speech likening major label practices to piracy, which typically left artists poorly paid, if paid at all (Gantz and Rochester 86). The surge of resistance to corporate control of music enabled by Napster stretched beyond the desires of music consumers, affecting producers as well.

Napster was ultimately crushed by recording industry lawsuits after a last-ditch alliance with German media company Bertelsmann.[4] In response, a slew of copycat programs sprung up in its wake. A rival file-sharing program, Gnutella, was constructed in a completely decentralized way: unlike Napster, not even the search inquiries were centralized. While this meant a slower network, Gnutella developers hoped it would insulate their software from legal liability for the kind of infringing user activity that took down Napster.[5] After America Online acquired

Gnutella, and subsequently shut it down due to piracy fears, hackers reverse-engineered the program and released open-source versions, which became the backbone for a number of popular P2P platforms. This proliferation of pirate platforms was so virulent that even when the RIAA successfully forced P2P company LimeWire to dismantle its networks, a "pirate version" of the program quickly emerged that even LimeWire itself was helpless to stop (Sandoval). A more perfect example of Rediker and Linebaugh's hydra metaphor would be difficult to come by. These insurgencies did not emerge from the technology of the Internet itself, but from the work and organization of hackers and pirates, struggling to maintain systems by which files could be exchanged noncommercially.

Pirates themselves have used this hydra metaphor to describe their tactics. The proprietors of the Pirate Bay, the most popular public tracker for users of the BitTorrent protocol,[6] took an explicitly antagonistic stance against the content industries, going so far as to publicly post takedown notices along with their profanity-laced responses. Rather than searching for Silicon Valley success, the Pirate Bay explicitly rejected commercialization, and hearkened back to the displays of transgression that characterized the warez Scene. However, the Pirate Bay's singular prominence was never the goal. On his blog, Pirate Bay co-founder Peter Sunde (brokep) put out a call for further decentralization of torrent trackers: "public message to people – start up your own torrent sites, make the internet the hydra it is and needs to be. If there's hundreds of sites, they can't all be shut down." The hydra describes the tactical structure of the informal organization of pirates.

With BitTorrent and the Pirate Bay, 2007 proved to be a high-water mark for the piratical Internet. According to Internet researchers at ipoque, 70% of global Internet usage came from P2P that year. To a large extent, this was because the BitTorrent protocol's ability to handle large files meant that piracy no longer focused on the bite-sized pieces of content represented by MP3s, but could now tackle larger media: entire feature films. The creation of a noncommercial ecosystem of media goods was, for a time, a success. As Andersson describes it in his analysis of The Pirate Bay, "The tactical nature of consumption is in other words increasingly replaced by more strategic instantiations of distribution and consumption, as the users themselves take more control and a new order gains permanence" (67). Digital piracy became a widespread accepted practice, even as systems repeatedly fell to content industry lawsuits.

Streaming: Recomposition and Formalization

Capital did not simply decompose the pirate threat by shutting down its servers and prosecuting participants. It also recuperated piratical activity by treating pirates not only as criminals, but also as a new kind of audience. However, the notoriously technologically phobic recording industry, which had scuttled or hamstrung a number of digital music initiatives, was not the driver of this change. Rather, the technology company Apple successfully commodified MP3s with the iTunes store. Apple had been a major beneficiary of the rise of the pirate MP3 ecosystem, which, in turn, drove the sale of the iPod playback device and other technologies involving the new capacities opened by digital media.

Transforming pirate commodities like MP3s into legitimate ones via iTunes was still not enough to contain piracy. MP3s could be recirculated through pirate channels, even when purchased legitimately. Attempts to insert copy protections into MP3s – so-called "Digital Rights Management systems" – were unpopular failures. Instead, another technique pioneered by pirates would provide the cultural industries with the means to reassert control over media distribution.

In 2010, ipoque reported that BitTorrent traffic had shrunk slightly, while streaming media, coming from "cyberlocker" sites like RapidShare and Megaupload, had grown rapidly. These sites did not use the bandwidth or hard drive space of users to circulate files; instead, files were hosted on the company's servers, encrypted in an attempt to insulate the companies from charges that they enabled piracy. This was a reassertion of a "client-server" model of distribution: while users uploaded files, Megaupload's servers hosted all content and served all streaming requests. As Nick Marx describes it, they "remove the direct P2P element from file sharing and reinsert a distribution intermediary between industry and consumer." With this intermediary status came the ability to monetize traffic, particularly through advertising.

Ramon Lobato places cyberlockers and linking sites at the midpoint between the informal and extralegal P2P piracy and formal and legal services like iTunes: cyberlockers can host files in legitimate and legal ways, but also contain loads of illegal content. "The rise of grey intermediaries... [throws] into the mix a new set of commercial and putatively legal services which work to *deformalise* online media markets while also opening up new commercial spaces and lines of business" (97). As a result, "cockroach capitalists" like Kim Dotcom, proprietor of Megaupload, reaped enormous profits through the grey economy of streaming before prosecutions tied up his wealth.

But major companies operate in ways startlingly similar to cockroaches like Dotcom. While much scholarship and discourse on YouTube emphasizes its user-generated fare and participatory network of amateurs, the site is "financially reliant on commercially produced content" even though most of this content is unauthorized (Lobato 102). Because of its centralized architecture, as long as YouTube responds quickly to DMCA takedown requests by rights holders, it avoids lawsuits, even though it has strong incentives for copyright infringement. "The key to survival in this part of the online distribution economy is to make your service as attractive as possible to users (including illegal uploaders) while placating regulators and rights-holders by removing this content when requested" (ibid).[7] In Lobato's estimation, the implementation of Content Identification systems, view counters, data collection, and monetization options represent an effort to formalize what had been a largely informal means of distribution.

Yet this was a one-sided formalization. As streaming sites moved toward legal legitimacy by obeying intellectual property laws and adhering to requirements set by rights holders, they continued to rely on a largely informal labor force: invisible to the state and most regulations, with obedience or understanding of intellectual property laws, and having little recourse to compensation. Most YouTube uploaders will make no money from the audiences they provide to the site; even those who attempt to monetize their uploaded content are subject to a shifting terrain of legality and obligation that can by no means be understood as formal. YouTube itself states on its site that "There are no guarantees under the YouTube partner agreement about how much, or whether, you will be paid." Users face constantly changing terms of service, unexplained and unjustified takedowns, opacity in payment systems, and a general lack of responsiveness that would characterize a formal employment relationship. Uploaders are referred to as "partners," interpellating these workers, pirate and legitimate, as entrepreneurs, though without any ownership rights. If content is found to be infringing, YouTube can simply disavow the pirate's labor, while keeping any profits generated beforehand.

Wholly formalized streaming services have now emerged, explicitly aimed at cutting off pirate venues. According to Daniel Ek, the founder of music-streaming service Spotify (and once the CEO of BitTorrent client uTorrent), "Spotify's primary objective is to migrate illegal file-sharers to its service, shifting 15–25 year old music fans to a legal model that puts money back into the creation of new music" (14). These are part of a larger music distribution technique called "Music as a Service": the model whereby "distribution coincides with the consumption," thereby outflanking piracy, which usurps legitimate distribution (Dörr et al. 385). Because no music is stored, issues of the usage rights of audiences, such as fair use, never come into play.

Instead, users pay for time to access archives of music. In this way, streaming is a rentier model, which relies upon continuous access to the servers – which is also to say, it relies on the company's continuous access to the listener. This "celestial jukebox" as Burkart and McCourt call it, potentially limits music's role as a cultural practice, turning it into another arm of passive consumption and data aggregation by tethering all user behavior to corporate servers, euphemistically referred to as "the cloud."

The cloud, whether pirate or legitimate, functions to decompose the P2P masses, recomposing them as an atomized audience, one that is also a digital labor force that produces large amounts of data. In fact, streaming models perfect the reach of market research: all consumer behavior can be tracked: time, place, duration, and so on. And this model has proven to be successful: Netflix, a legitimate streamer, has replaced BitTorrent as the largest single chunk of bandwidth in the US and is now a major producer of cinematic content.

To conclude, the history of digital piracy shows that pirate labor and its struggles have been the motive force in transforming the Internet into a media distribution platform. The process by which capital has attempted to formalize this distribution has been tremendously conflict-ridden and contradictory. Corporate demands push up against existing cultural practices, different sectors of capital compete for control over new markets, and piracy remains a specter haunting the orderly exchange of commodities online. Capital has successively domesticated the online environment by decomposing the pirate threat, via attacking its organization (prosecuting individual pirates, seizing equipment) as well as developing new forms of technology to outflank piracy. In an ironic twist, pirates themselves have been part of this innovation.

Notes

1 Cracktros spun off into the "demoscene," where programmers created "demos" of computer animation and music, without any direct connection to piracy. The demoscene continues to thrive today, particularly in Scandinavia. See Reunanen.

2 This is an instructive analogy. The home auto mechanic, a masculine emblem of autonomy and self-sufficiency, reliant on skill, stands opposed to crass commercial interests.

3 This is strongly reminiscent of the "eternal September," when existing net users had to suddenly deal with an influx of novice users due to the success of America Online. Previously, online communities only had to deal with waves of new users during the month of September, as college students used university systems to connect to the Internet. See Grossman's *net.wars*.

4 After the Napster deal, Bertelsmann would be subject to lawsuits from rights holders for years to come ("Napster and Bertelsmann: It Seemed Like A Good Idea").

5 It would not: in the 2005 Grokster case, the Supreme Court ruled that even decentralized and noncommercial software could be found liable for "inducement" (Sinnreich 14).

6 The BitTorrent protocol is, chiefly, a way to make P2P file sharing more efficient and stable, by dividing files into pieces which can be downloaded from a host of peers. A tracker locates these pieces, acting as a broker between peers, though without ever hosting the file itself.

7 One can only speculate that YouTube has avoided the fate of RapidShare and Megaupload due to its patronage by the Google.

Works Cited

Alderman, John. *Sonic Boom: Napster, MP3, and the New Pioneers of Music.* New York, NY: Basic Books, 2001.

Andersson, Jonas. "For the Good of the Net: The Pirate Bay as Strategic Sovereign." *Culture Machine* 10 (2009): 64–108.

"BeatForge." *Mp3scene.* n. pag, n.d. Web. 14 June 2014.

Benjamin, Walter. "The Author as Producer." *New Left Review* No. 62 (July–Aug. 1970).

———. "The Work of Art in the Age of Mechanical Reproduction." Trans. Harry Zohn. *Marxists Internet Archive.* 1998. Web. 13 June, 2014.

Burkart, Peter and Tom McCourt. *Digital Music Wars: Ownership and Control of the Celestial Jukebox.* Lanham, MD: Rowman & Littlefield Publishers, 2006.

Cherki, Eddy and Michel Wieviorka. "Autoreduction Movements in Turin." *Autonomia: Post-Political Politics.* Eds. Sylvere Lotringer and Christian Marazzi. Los Angeles, CA: Semiotext(e), 2007. 72–78.

"Cracking Tips (Part 1)." *Pirate.* 1990. Web. Accessed June 14, 2014.

Décary-Hetu, David, Carlo Morselli, and Stéphane Leman-Langlois. "Welcome to the Scene: A Study of Social Organization and Recognition among Warez Hackers." *Journal of Research in Crime and Delinquency* 49 (2012): 359–382.

Dörr, Jonathan, Thomas Wagner, Alexander Benlian, and Thomas Hess. "Music as a Service as an Alternative to Music Piracy?" *Business & Information Systems Engineering* 5.6 (Dec. 2013): 383–396.

Ek, Daniel. "Spot and Identify." *IFPI Digital Music Report 2010.* London: IFPI, 2010. 14.

Gantz, John and Jack B. Rochester. *Pirates of the Digital Millennium.* Upper Saddle River, NJ: Financial Times Prentice Hall, 2005.

Gillespie, Tarleton. *Wired Shut: Copyright and the Shape of Digital Culture.* Cambridge, MA: The MIT P, 2009.

Goldman, Eric. "A Road to No Warez: The No Electronic Theft Act and Criminal Copyright Infringement." *Oregon Law Review* 82 (2003): 369–432.

Guzman, Andrea L. and Steve Jones. "Napster and the Press: Framing Music Technology." *First Monday* 19.10 (6 Oct. 2014). Web. 13 Apr. 2015.

Haight, Bev. "They Don't Want their Readers to Back Up 'Protected' Disks!: Censorship in Computer Magazines." *Hardcore Computing* 1.1 (1981): 1–6.

Hargadon, Michael A. "Like City Lights, Receding: ANSi Artwork and the Digital Underground, 1985–2000." Master's thesis, Concordia University, 2001.

Heneghan, Brian P. "The NET Act, Fair Use, and Willfulness – Is Congress Making a Scarecrow of the Law?" *Journal of High Technology Law* 1.1 (2002): 27–46.

Howe, Jeff. "The Shadow Internet." *Wired* 13.1 (2005): Web. 14 June 2014.

Huizing, Ard and Jan A. van der Wal. "Explaining the Rise and Fall of the Warez MP3 Scene: An Empirical Account from the Inside." *First Monday* 19.10 (6 Oct. 2014). Web. 13 Apr. 2015.

"Interview with NetFrack." *Affinity* 3 (19 Aug. 1996). Web. 14 June 2014.

Ipoque. "Internet Study 2007." n.p. 2007. Web. 14 June 2014.

———. "Internet Study 2010." n.p., 2010. Web. 14 June 2014.

Karaganis, Joe. "Rethinking Piracy." *Media Piracy in Emerging Economies.* Ed. Joe Karaganis. Brooklyn, NY: SSRC, 2011.

Kelty, Chris. *Two Bits: The Cultural Significance of Free Software.* Durham, NC: Duke UP, 2008.

Kleiner, Dmytri. *The Telekommunist Manifesto.* Amsterdam: Colophon, 2010.

Kline, Stephen, Nick Dyer-Witheford, and Greig de Peuter. *Digital Play: The Interaction of Technology, Culture, and Marketing.* Montreal: McGill-Queen's UP, 2003.

Lessig, Lawrence. *Code and Other Laws of Cyberspace.* New York, NY: Basic Books, 1999.

Lieberman, David. "States Settle CD Rice-Fixing Case." *USA Today.* 30 Sept. 2002.

Linebaugh, Peter and Marcus Rediker. *The Many-Headed Hydra: Sailors, Slaves, Commoners, and the Hidden History of the Revolutionary Atlantic.* Boston, MA: Beacon P, 2005.

Lobato, Ramon. *Shadow Economies of Cinema: Mapping Informal Film Distribution.* London: British Film Institute, 2012.

Marx, Nick. "Storage Wars: Clouds, Cyberlockers, and Media Piracy in the Digital Economy." *E-Media Studies* 3.1 (2013), n. pag. Web. 13 Apr. 2015.

Menn, Joseph. *All the Rave: The Rise and Fall of Shawn Fanning's Napster.* New York, NY: Crown, 2003.

Merriden, Trevor. *Irresistible Forces: The Business Legacy of Napster and the Growth of the Underground Internet.* Mankato, MN: Capstone Publishers, 2001.

"Napster and Bertelsmann: It Seemed Like A Good Idea..." *Bloomberg*, 2 Aug. 2004. Web. 14 June 2014.

"Prince Backs 'exciting' Napster." *BBC News.* 10 Aug. 2000. Web. 17 Aug. 2014.

"A Recap of the MP3 Scene, From the RIAA 2013 Ruleset." *mp3Scene* n.p., n.d. Web. 14 June 2014.

Reunanen, Markku. "How Those Crackers Became Us Demosceners." *WiderScreen* 1–2 (2014): n. pag. Web. 13 June 2014.

Sandoval, Greg. "RIAA Wants Revived LimeWire Dead and Buried." *CNet*. 19 Nov. 2010. Web. 13 Dec. 2015.

Sinnreich, Aram. *The Piracy Crusade: How the Music Industry's War on Sharing Destroys Markets and Erodes Civil Liberties*. Amherst: U of Massachusetts P, 2013.

Smith, Andrew. "A Guide to Internet Piracy." *2600: Hacker Quarterly* 21.2 (2004). Web. 14 June, 2014.

"So You Want to Be a Pirate?" 1989. *Pirate*. Web. Accessed June 14, 2014.

Söderberg, Johan. "Misuser Inventions and the Invention of the Misuser: Hackers, Crackers and Filesharers." *Science as Culture* 19.2(2010): 151–179. Spangler, Todd. "Pirated Copy of 'Walter Mitty' Surfaces Online with 'Ellen DeGeneres' Watermark." *Variety*. 2014. Web. 14 June 2014.

Sterne, Jonathan. *MP3: The Meaning of a Format*. Durham, NC: Duke UP, 2012.

Sunde, Peter. "PrivacySpy." *Copy Me Happy*. 26 June 2007. Web. 12 June 2014.

Thomas, Douglas. *Hacker Culture*. Minneapolis: U of Minnesota P, 2003.

Thomas, Jim and Gordon Meyer. "Software Piracy: An Alternative View." *Computer Underground Digest* 1.03 (1990). Web. 14 June 2014.

4   Theorizing Piracy

Piracy has proven a difficult concept to theorize. This is, to a great extent, due to the extremely moralizing discourse surrounding the unauthorized circulation of files online, leading to a pitched propaganda war between content industries and digital rights activists. In this chapter, I seek to theorize piracy as an existing social practice, rather than a deviant behavior or a heroic act. Further, I situate this social practice as a complex and contradictory political formation within the context of contemporary capitalism. In what follows, I offer a critical analysis of prior attempts to describe the political and economic content, both latent and explicit, in online piracy.

Schumpeterian Perspectives

One influential theorization of piracy envisions it as an insurgent frontier of new forms of capitalism. In this telling, the criminalization of certain forms of commerce and exchange is merely a method for established actors to maintain their hold over the production and circulation of commodities in the face of challenges from new, nimble, technologically adept actors. Matt Mason's *Pirate's Dilemma* is a perfect example of such a theorization. After the book's release, Mason worked to reorient the image and strategy of BitTorrent, a company that administers the eponymous file-sharing protocol, meaning that his views are highly relevant to the conception of piracy's relationship to politics, technology, and economics.

According to Mason, piracy heralds the arrival of "Punk Capitalism," "the new set of market conditions governing society. It's a society where piracy, as the cochair at Disney recently put it, is 'just another business model'" (8). Crucial to Punk Capitalism are "[d]isruptive new D.I.Y. technologies [which] are causing unprecedented creative destruction" (12). Here, then, is the invocation of political economist Joseph

Schumpeter, a beloved figure among Silicon Valley business gurus (Mason approving cites Schumpeter a few pages later). In this account, capitalist crises are caused by the arrival of disruptive innovations, new technologies, and methods that threaten existing capitalist practices, a process Schumpeter referred to as "creative destruction":

> The opening up of new markets, foreign or domestic, and the organizational development from the craft shop to such concerns as U.S. Steel illustrate the same process of industrial mutation – if I may use that biological term – that incessantly revolutionizes the economic structure from within, incessantly destroying the old one, incessantly creating a new one. This process of Creative Destruction is the essential fact about capitalism. (83)

Schumpeter, by his own admission, was deeply influenced by Marx's account in the *Communist Manifesto* of capitalism's tendency to "constantly revolutionize the means of production." However, rather than align with Marxist politics, he set himself the task to combat the arrival of socialism (see Elliott 47). Rather than systematically dismantle Marx's analysis, Schumpeter adopts much of Marx wholesale, arguing that technological revolutions and the upheavals they cause are at the core of capitalism:

> the competition from the new commodity, the new technology, the new source of supply, the new type of organization (the largest-scale unit of control for instance) – competition which commands a decisive cost or quality advantage and which strikes not at the margins of the profits and the outputs of the existing firms but at their foundations and their very lives. (84)

This is Mason's perspective as well. Piracy is the unwanted competition from new technologies, such as peer-to-peer file sharing and remixing, and new types of organization, such as file-sharing communities, that are unwanted competition for established businesses.

> By short-circuiting conventional channels and red tape, pirates can deliver new materials, formats, and business models to audiences who want them.... Piracy transforms the markets it operates in, changing the way distribution works and forcing companies to be more competitive and innovative. (38)

Piracy, then, is just another name for this incipient technological revolution, which is subsequently criminalized in an effort to preserve market position: "But we are losing our rights and innovation is being stifled

because companies using outdated business models and inefficient distribution systems don't want to switch to the new formats people are being
criminalized for using" (61). In this account, piracy is not simply progress,
but justice: it has a moral element. This parts ways with Schumpeter, who
did not believe that even large firms could resist creative destruction:
"a monopoly position is in general no cushion to sleep on" (102).

Mason identifies piracy as not merely technological, but a cultural
logic linked to new labor structures: "Jobs are radically changing because of this shift in the way the labor force is operating, and the idea
of the work/life balance is being replaced by a new discussion on what
work and life as separate entities actually means" (26). Mason seems
to gesture toward the flexibilization and casualization of employment
discussed in Chapter 1. However, the impetus for the transition in
work has more to do with Do-It-Yourself (DIY) anti-corporate sensi-
bilities, linked to youth cultures such as hip hop, rave, and street art of
which piracy is a part. "The exponential growth of self-employment
isn't just about sticking it the man on a global scale. It reflects a
deeper change in our attitudes" (ibid). While Mason's theorization
is an admirable break with technological determinism, it substitutes
countercultural values – that young people adopt piracy as a DIY
lifestyle choice – for large-scale economic transformations fails to
hold up under scrutiny.

In *Piracy*, historian Adrian Johns offers a detailed historical
account of intellectual property violations, casting them in a similarly
Schumpeterian light. Pirates repeatedly disrupt, via entrepreneurial
moxy and technological prowess, such tightly controlled industries as
book publishing, music printing, and terrestrial radio. However, the
threats posed by piracy are as much about social control as they are
about economics: "Printing posed serious problems of politics and
authority for the generations following Gutenberg," he states (8). The
piratical protagonists of his vignettes are motivated as much by political problems over the control of knowledge as strictly profit-oriented
concerns. It is, then, not capitalist imperatives, such as those described by libertarian economist Peter Leeson, who argues in *The
Invisible Hook* that historical pirates were rational utility maximiz-
ers. Rather, it is a moral economy, a term Johns repeatedly returns
to in his analysis of pirate motivations and arguments. Yet elsewhere,
Johns pegs this moral economy to a specific political viewpoint. In
his description of pirate philosophy, Johns claims that the ideology
of pirates "is a moral philosophy through and through…. it has to do
centrally with convictions about freedom, rights, duties, obligations,
and the like. In many cases these are tackled in a frankly libertarian
framework" (46).

Schumpeterian theorizing of piracy seizes upon two related phenomena: the arbitrariness of the distinction between piracy and legitimate forms of conduct, and the impact of this distinction on market relations. The former is summed up well by historian Frederic L. Cheyette's analysis of privateering: "it is not the act that renders itself legitimate, nor the actor, but the authorization" (quoted in Heller-Roazen 81). Privateers and pirates both engaged in looting of merchant ships, but only with the possession of a document of sovereign authorization – known as a patent – would the act be protected by law. As the term "piracy" was extended to violations of intellectual property, it marked the distinction between legitimate commerce and illegitimate commerce, one which rested upon state sanction: ultimately arbitrary and, therefore, unjust administrative fiat.

Schumpeterian viewpoints have the good sense to locate piracy within a crisis of state and economy, where the state meets resistance to regulations over market exchange. They correctly identify the extensions of control over a distributed productive apparatus by entrenched capitalists, using both the state and technology. Indeed, one virtue of their perspective is to examine piracy as a question, not of consumption, but of production and distribution of commodities. However, they mistake piracy as largely a rhetorical and juridical category whose primary purpose is to discipline competitors. If only free competition were permitted, they suggest, everyone would benefit, except inefficient industries. This is, in part, because of the neoclassical methodological framework, which situates itself epistemologically from a rationally maximizing individual consumer who is negatively impacted by "overregulation" and a lack of innovation. While it makes for an easy story to tell, it neglects the larger contradictions in 21st-century capitalism that the term "piracy" signifies.

Capitalism contains numerous contradictions internal to its own workings. To explain a crisis in terms of an autochthonous technological development, a "disruptive innovation," is to ignore how technological developments themselves emerge from capitalism's imperatives, contradictions, and crises. Taking this into account, it becomes clear that piratical practices and technologies do not solve capitalist problems – pirates are not heroes in a unilinear narrative of progress, efficiency, and consumer demand – but are complex and contradictory. Further, most piracy is not entrepreneurial activity per se, but, as described previously, a complex array of practices where economic, political, and cultural concerns come into play. Contra Schumpeterians, piracy is not the solution to a crisis: it is the crisis itself.

Piracy as Reform

Studies that view piracy from a political viewpoint, rather than economic competitors *in potentia*, come to very different conclusions as to its effects in conflicts at the level of state and cultural economy. In his study of the Swedish Pirate Party, sociologist Peter Burkart locates the politics of piracy in the reaction to overreach by corporations and states, a dialectic which he theorizes in Habermasian terms. "The SPP expresses the cultural shock of 'lifeworld structures' confronting expanded markets, bureaucratic-technical processes, and police powers" (11). This shock is translated into a "vision of an alternative information age based on the public domain and the intellectual and cultural commons" (23). Burkart posits file sharing as potentially a communicative act "that communicates in-group or intersubjective solidarity and political arousal," and even when not consciously political, "a variety of lifeworld experience shared by more and more people who are participating in media urbanism" (29). Without file sharing, cybercultures do not exist, and any attempt to limit this provokes an attempt to protect the culture.

This echoes the more Deleuzian-inflected theorization of Rodolphe Durand and Jean-Phillippe Vergne, who attempt to extend Heller-Roazen's discussion of sovereignty with a consideration of capitalism. They define capitalism as dependent on a dynamic of "deterritorialization and normalization" (18). It is a twofold movement of "on the one hand, the deterritorialization of capital, resources, and labor, and their reterritorialization into the trade space; on the other hand, the normalization of this trade space through the definition and enforcement of norms that delineate legitimate exchanges" (22). Essentially, when capitalism expands into new realms, it must deterritorialize existing relations and reterritorialize according to its norms of exchange, thus expanding sovereignty. This expansion meets inevitable pushback from actors labeled "pirates" or other kinds of criminals.

According to Durand and Vergne, "the pirate organization does not seek to overthrow and replace the system in place; rather, it seeks to challenge widespread norms" (55): it is ultimately a reformist struggle for the maintenance of prior practices. The push and pull between the sovereign and the pirate organization means that "[n]orms of exchange and competition are thus constantly redefined as the sovereign decides to keep in or out elements of the public cause defended and embodied by pirate organizations" (121). While often abstract to the point of vagueness, their perspective aligns with Burkart's argument that pirate organizations "represent a new middle-class interest in preserving dominant social institutions, including capitalism, as well as privileged positions within them" (30).

Analyses such as Burkart's offer a more explicit sociological explanation of the social base of initiatives such as Lawrence Lessig's battles against copyright: they are, at bottom, middle-class reform movements; in Burkart's terms, "loyal opposition to the Celestial Jukebox" (51). But like Lessig, such a perspective relies on circumscribing whose activity is properly political. Burkart's study largely limits itself to specific activist-oriented initiatives and Pirate Party statements, thus neglecting a wider world of practice that is not easily integrated into the notion of a lifeworld or a single online community. Burkart presents a compelling view of conscious activists, which, however, leaves out a large portion of those engaged in piracy by examining the most vocal activists as the representatives of piracy as a whole.[1] And while he gives an excellent account of the larger political and economic context of these actors, Burkart fails to offer a political theory that encompasses the totality of piracy. To a great extent, his conclusions are colored by the selection of the object of research. A political party formed on the basis of a few interrelated demands, such as the Swedish Pirate Party, will necessarily appear reformist; a reformist line in the midst of nominal social democracy will necessarily appear to promote social democracy. However, a more detailed contextualization of piracy from within its economic context reveals a different kind of politics, one not always formalized or consciously espoused, but emerging more symptomatically and antagonistically.

Piracy and Acceleration

Sociologist Jonas Andersson Schwartz dissents with Burkart's characterization of file sharers as part of a *Gemeinschaft*, and finds little evidence that the broader public shares their views. Rather than reformists, Schwartz analyzes pirates using the political concept of *accelerationism*:

> Rather than halting the onslaught of capital (such as by defending the welfare state or defending the right to work), accelerationism is a philosophical and political strategy that strives to exacerbate its processes to bring forth its inner contradictions and thereby hasten its destruction, to accelerate them beyond the control of the established gatekeepers of capitalism. (20)

For Schwartz, "Illegal file sharing can be said to be accelerationist in that it challenges the capitalist system by over-affirming it" (21). In other words, file sharing represents the acceleration of consumer desire for media products, a desire engendered by the culture industry itself that also threatens to undermine it. The contradiction emerges, not from the productive forces themselves, but from the self-activity of consumers. This account aligns with the historical record of piracy: while capital developed the breakthrough pirate technology of the MP3, it was pirate users who developed its usage for home-based media distribution and consumption through free software and file-sharing protocols.

Schwartz's conclusions are the opposite of Burkart's: digital pirate politics are essentially libertarian, not social democratic. The morals and ethics of file sharers are "premised on the diagrams of networked individualism and networked accumulation... To argue for file sharing to be entirely unrestricted is very much to argue for borderless competition – laissez-faire economics" (81). Examining the debates over piracy in Sweden, Schwartz detects a Hayekian flavor, an ideology more characteristic of US technolibertarianism than Swedish approaches to politics: "Swedish cyberliberties activism turns primarily on the individual rather than the (traditional) collective... the benefit to the collective is thought chiefly as a by-product of the individual benefit" (117).

The link between piracy, digitization, and speed is compelling, but rather than articulated purely in a voluntaristic mode, can be analyzed symptomatically, as emerging from the dynamics of post-Fordist capitalism. One of the more impressive attempts to do this is Atle Kjøsen's master's thesis "An Accident of Value." For Kjøsen, piracy emerges from a contradiction within capitalism. Capitalism endeavors to accelerate its accumulation cycle, but this same "need for speed" also threatens its own stability (10). What Kjøsen ventures is that digital networks dramatically accelerate circulation such that capital is unable to travel through its necessary stages, thereby undermining the commodity form. In this way, piracy is a side effect of a contradiction in capitalism. Standing as one of the few sustained Marxist theorizations of digital piracy, this argument is worth unpacking.

As Kjøsen reminds us, capital exists not as a static thing, but comes into view in the process of circulation. Combining labor-power with the means of production produces commodities, which are sold, and the profits invested in new rounds of production. Speeding up this cycle, i.e. reducing turnover time, expands the profits of the capitalist. Hence, any lags in time in this circuit, any points where capital finds itself frozen in one of its forms, appear as a loss potential value that must be transcended or circumvented.

> Circulation time in itself is not a *productive force of capital*, but *a barrier to its productive force* arising from its nature as exchange value. The passage through the various phases of circulation

here appears as *a barrier to production*, a barrier posited by the specific nature of capital itself. (Marx, *Grundrisse* 545, italics in original)

Kjøsen argues that digital piracy is "an accident of value": an "occurrence that stops or slows down the flow of value and/or causes the circuit to leak value" (69–70). This specific accident occurs as capital attempts to speed up its circulation time, reducing it to zero. However, circulation time is a necessary component in capitalist production. As Marx states in the *Grundrisse*,

the nature of capital presupposes that it travels through the different phases of circulation not as it does in the mind, where one concept turns into the next at the speed of thought, in no time, but rather as situations which are separate in time. It must spend some time as a cocoon before it can take off as a butterfly. (548)

Kjøsen argues that digital piracy in effect overturns Marx's metaphor: commodities become butterflies – that is, consumed – immediately upon production, circumventing exchange, and therefore, causing a crisis in accumulation of profits.

Kjøsen's account, drawing on Marx and Paul Virilio, is theoretically sophisticated, and evinces a nuanced understanding of digital technologies. The digital does represent a substantial acceleration in the circulation of commodities. However, it is not clear that this acceleration itself can shake apart the commodity form: after all, digital commodities do exist. To distinguish between legitimate digital commodities, such as those on iTunes or provided through streaming services, Kjøsen makes a distinction between immediacy, which features "a brief temporal lag, even if only a fraction of a second" (77), and simultaneity, which contains absolutely no lag: "In byte-size, the commodity assumes a form, which, like electronic money and credit, is identical to the speed of transmission" (78). Legitimate services can be commodified because of that fraction of a second, which maintains a schema where production and circulation are distinct.

Yet this technicality does not hold up to scrutiny. Many commodities are produced at the moment they are consumed: those which fall under the category of "service." The production of, say, a lecture, is simultaneously its consumption by students, but this does not rule out the ability to commodify education.[2] Furthermore, the circulation of digital commodities is never instantaneous. As the high-frequency trading industry shows, small differences in the length of fiber-optic cables lead to different transfer times. These are fractions of seconds, but they determine which trading algorithm has access to the most up-to-date stock market information, and minute efficiencies are highly sought after (Adler). All of this is to say that the speed of light – the speed at which electrons travel through fiber-optic cables – is, after all, still a speed.[3]

Kjøsen's account needs supplementing by more careful attention to what occurs in the sphere of circulation, and what effects digital technologies have on cultural economies. The transformation of circulation is marked, as is post-Fordism more generally, by dynamics of automation, deskilling, and the subsequent restructuring of cultural labor along formally subsumed lines. I will examine how these forces impact circulation, and theorize the relationship of this to the insertion of legal barriers – what Kjøsen likens to speed bumps.

Much of Marx's discussion of circulation is located in Volume 2 of *Capital*. In its sixth chapter, Marx details the points in the circulation of commodities where surplus value is added. These constitute "production processes that are simply continued in the circulation sphere, and whose productive character is thus merely hidden by the circulation form" (214): in other words, they are productive processes, even though they occur at the stage of circulation, not the stage of direct production of the commodity. These processes include the transportation and storage of commodities; they appear unproductive because they do not add use value to the commodities, but "for the individual capitalist they can constitute sources of enrichment" due to a reliance on living labor and the effect on the overall value of the commodities this labor performs (ibid).

> The persistence of commodity capital as a commodity stock requires buildings, stores, containers, warehouses, i.e. an outlay of constant capital; it equally requires that payment be made for the labour-power employed in placing the commodities in their containers. Furthermore, commodities decay, and are subject to the damaging influence of the elements. Additional capital must thus be expended to protect them from this, partly in objective form as means of labour, and partly in labour-power. (215–6)

Here Marx notes the two expenses incurred by capitalists are, as always, cost of fixed capital (instruments of labor) and cost of variable capital (wages for labor power). This is the same relationship at work in the direct production process:

> The productive capital invested in [the transportation] industry thus adds to the products transported, partly through the value carried over from the means of transport, partly through the value added by the work of transport. This latter addition of value can be divided, as with all capitalist production, into replacement of wages and surplus-value. (226–7)

Thus, the same dynamic that seeks to increase productivity in the interest of securing a greater share of surplus value for the capitalist is the same: mechanizing and automating as much of this work as possible. "The capitalist mode of production reduces the transport costs for the individual commodity by developing the means of transport and communication, as well as by concentrating transport – i.e. by increasing its scale" (228–9).

This dynamic was one of the major triumphs of digitalization of media. In the form of pure information, transportation costs could be reduced dramatically, and little living labor would be required for storage and transportation. Davis and Stack state that as digital commodities replace earlier forms, "so entire layers of human labor are evicted from production, warehousing, transportation and sales" (122). These reductions were already achieved with the development of the compact disc, which took up less space and held more information than cassettes, in addition to being cheaper to produce. However, it should be re-emphasized that the culture industries themselves (with the partial exception of software) resisted the move to full informatization of media. With few precedents for the sale of purely digital commodities, the culture industries balked at giving up the physical container form entirely.

The reduction of living labor required in the production of media commodities will lead, in Marx's account, to a reduction in the value of those commodities over time. Yet specific histories will vary. The culture industries reduced labor and material costs while *increasing* the price of their goods: at their peak, an audio CD cost double what a vinyl record had cost. As Kjøsen notes, "The transitions from one format to the next have been economically beneficial to the music industry as old recordings have been recycled in new formats and without major changes to the supply chain" (76). Due to the creation of an illegal cartel, the recording industry temporarily reaped superprofits, before online piratical practices became widespread.

This reveals the importance of copyright to the circulation of media commodities. To take one example, the recording industry functions by paying for fixed capital (in the form of recording studios, equipment, and the like) and the labor power of musicians and technicians. While some profit-sharing between artists and capital exists in the form of royalty payments to artists, these payments are, with few exceptions, small and relatively uncommon. Their function is primarily ideological, to portray capitalist and artist as partners, when in reality the company maintains ownership and rarely shares profit. The result of this arrangement is a recording. The recording, typically in the form of a master tape, is an element of fixed capital, deployed in the manufacture of objects such as discs. These end commodities are copies of the recording.

Only a copyright holder or licensee may legally produce these consumer objects. In this sense, a copyright is a restriction on production. The problem stemming from the transformation of cultural goods into digital objects (including optical discs) is that *the consumer object itself*, the recording, can be deployed as fixed capital, whether in a CD burner or in a hard drive, to create near-identical copies. This problem was not new, and had been mitigated in the case of previous forms of recordable media by allowing the culture industries to add a small surcharge to recordable media, such as blank tapes and discs. However, there is no mechanism for compensating purely digital products, although a number of "solutions" to piracy include a surcharge added to one's Internet Service Provider bill (Rose).

Industry-proposed regulations seek to limit production, indicating that, rather than enforce immediacy, anti-piracy initiatives seek to govern the productive process itself. Digital commodities are not exhausted in use, and thus they lead to an overaccumulation of commodities. There is no such thing as "out of print," and with the advent of long-tail distribution, where any past commodity is available to the consumer, cultural commodities compete with a vast accumulation of dead labor. This situation has come about in part due to the archives pioneered by pirates, and then emulated (in the case of iTunes) or outright appropriated (in the case of Google's purchase of YouTube, with its host of illegal content legitimated *ex post facto*). With the automation of distribution, there are no extra labor costs for shipping commodities, new or old, and very little in the way of technical costs, which had affected the way the music industry structured product cycles. In the past, shops could stock only a limited amount of commodities, and so they tended to prioritize new works with more marketing behind them. Now everything is more or less equally available. It is not merely that consumers who would have once bought a band's CD now pirate; it is also likely that consumers are listening to any number of past recordings.

Guard Labor

Focusing on the accelerationist component of piracy helps to explain its status as a unique kind of contemporary antagonism. Here state theorist Bob Jessop offers some suggestive remarks in light of late capitalism's acceleration. For Jessop, states require not just a spatial sovereignty, but a temporal one.

> States increasingly face temporal pressures in their policy-making and implementation due to new forms of time-space distantiation, compression, and differentiation. For example, as the temporal rhythms of the economy accelerate relative to those of the state, it has less time to determine and co-ordinate political responses to economic events, shocks, and crises. ("Marxist Approaches to State Power" 12)

Jessop lists three responses the state can take in response. Most frequently, it simply absconds from its duties and deregulates. It can also attempt to speed up its decision-making process, typically by vesting more power in less democratic organs, such as a unitary executive. Finally, it can attempt to "decelerate the activities of 'fast capitalism' to match existing political routines" (12).

The state response to piracy was to increase regulation, using the Digital Millennium Copyright Act designed by the culture industries, of which a major component was the accelerated (and undemocratic) decision-making processes, including automated takedown algorithms (see Carpou). These forces seek not only to discipline consumer behavior, but also to control productive activity. In the case of intellectual property, it is not merely that consumers should not illegally download, but that commodities, such as recordings, must not be put to use in production.

Techniques for controlling production, circulation, and consumption are commonplace in capitalism, particularly in periods of restructuring. These techniques themselves derive from a kind of work undertaken by human laborers. A useful examination of this phenomenon comes from a paper by economists Jayadev and Bowles, who label this concept "guard labor." While they present their research in the language of neoclassical economics, Jayadev and Bowles's analysis has striking parallels to Marxist theorizing of the economy. Their description of the economy in terms of employment is thus:

> Abstracting from the owners (and from those engaged in raising the next generation), the adult population in this economy consists of employed workers, monitors, unemployed workers, prisoners, guards, and military personnel. The first (employed workers) are productive in the sense that their effort is an argument of the firms' production functions. The efforts of the monitors, guards, and military personnel, by contrast, are directed not toward production, but toward the enforcement of claims arising from exchanges and the pursuit or prevention of unilateral transfers of property ownership. (335)

For Jayadev and Bowles, guard labor has a *political* function: "their common role in sustaining the status quo distribution of property rights and claims" (335). Michael Perelman provides a Marxist conceptualization of guard labor. "Capitalists are only able to market their goods to the extent that they can deny people access to goods without payment. Therefore, business must devote considerable effort just to protect its ownership" (10). According to Perelman, guard labor is not only management and literal guards, such as police and prison officials, but innocuous positions such as a theater ticket seller and a cashier. Guard labor is fundamentally about denying access to goods until the price has been paid, or in enforcing payment after goods have been delivered. In the digital context, this labor is also automated: digital rights management schemes, the insertion of passwords, and algorithms that predict and channel user behavior are forms of automated guard labor. The greater the acceleration, the more necessary these measures are, and the more likely for antagonism to break out into open contestation.

Piracy and Communization

The Swedish radical artistic and political collective Piratbyran (Swedish for "Pirate Bureau," a parody of the government's Antipiratbyran) offered their own theorization of piracy in terms of radical anti-capitalism.[4] There is an accelerationist flavor to the statements Schwartz records from the Piratbyran site: "The best strategy is to keep file sharing, sampling, deriving, copying, getting better broadband connections/'mp3-players' so that we become even more dependent on these phenomena and our actions make copyright so washed out that it is no longer needed" (129). By overidentifying with the features of the cultural economy of digital capitalism, internal contradictions will ultimately collapse the system.

In Piratbyran's account, P2P emerges in antagonism to a similarly deterministic one-way model for media transmission in the culture industries. It is a "counterprocess of primitive borderless accumulation outside the established monetary economy" responding to the primitive accumulation of increasingly restrictive copyright (130). Piracy crashes the gates of rentier enclosures, though what happens after – a reassertion of commodity exchange and capitalist competition, as neoclassical Schumpeterians would have it, or a transformation in the social relations of media production and consumption, as Piratbyran desires – is not decided in advance.

Piratbyran's theorization puts them on similar footing with insurrectionary ultraleft theoretical formations gathered under the classification of "communization," such as the Invisible Committee, Endnotes, and Théorie Communiste.[5] These tendencies have set themselves to the task of rediscovering and amplifying the forms taken by contemporary class struggle, regardless of stated politics or institutional affiliation – indeed, they seem to be attracted to movements where explicit politics are absent. These currents are directly inspired by Marx's remark at the end of the first section of *The German Ideology*:

> Communism is for us not a state of affairs which is to be established, an ideal to which reality [will] have to adjust itself. We call communism the real movement which abolishes the present state of things. The conditions of this movement result from the premises now in existence. (187)

Rather than a political platform or utopian end-goal, communism manifests itself as a dynamic and unfolding *movement* by proletarians aimed at the abolition of capitalist social relations. To capture this sense of movement, the term "communization" underscores communism as the content of struggle, and emphasizes immediate transition from capitalism to communism. As Ben Noys frames it, "communization suggests communism as a particular activity and process" where relevant struggles are "immediate, immanent, and as anti-identity" (8). Communization groups maintain a general hostility to putative working-class organizations such as trade unions and labor parties, which channel struggle into reformist institutions and historically have served the purpose of stabilizing crisis-ridden capitalism, rather than abolishing it.[6]

The Invisible Committee's *The Coming Insurrection* continues to receive the most attention of any communization group, likely due to its breathless millenarian language (its profile is such that right-wing talk show host Glenn Beck has featured it on his show). This manifesto seeks to recuperate and celebrate rebellious acts, placing them in a constellation of emergent class struggle that transcends the workplace. Instead of assuming a positive identity as a worker finding comrades on the shop floor, insurgents find one another through "everyday insubordination" (66). Crime is depicted as "a necessary disposition towards fraud" required to live outside of wage labor (69). Plunder becomes the basis for the creation of new forms of social reproduction: "Every practice brings a territory into existence... the more territories there are superimposed on a given zone, the more circulation there is between them, the harder it will be for power to get a handle on them" (72). This is a similar logic to Piratbyran's insistence that pirates keep copying and sharing.

This is, perhaps, the most romantic version of communization, akin to the Temporary Autonomous Zones described by Hakim Bey. Noys points to the parallels between *The Coming Insurrection* and radical theory drawing from "the common," where the immediate task is to prefigure communism by attempting to live it, even while surrounded on all sides by capitalist social relations in the form of wage labor, commodification, and the state. A number of scholars examining digital cultures have viewed them in terms of commons: that they are "gift economies," alternative islands in a sea of capitalism, where goods are exchanged without payment. Richard Barbrook's estimation is representative: these "hi-tech gift economies" represent an "anarcho-communist" subculture that subsists in a symbiotic relationship to capitalism. Gary Hall sounds a similar note:

> what is interesting is the potential pirate philosophy contains for the development of a new kind of economy and society: one based far less on individualism, possession, acquisition, accumulation, competition, celebrity, and ideas of knowledge, research and thought as something to be owned, commodified, communicated, disseminated and exchanged as the property of single, indivisible authors. (39)

Here the realization of an alternate framework of exchange destabilizes a host of other ideologies and practices thought to be essential to the reproduction of capitalism: the new society is borne in the fissures and gaps of the old. Yet it should be noted that the exchange of

pirate goods does not follow the same logic as the gift economies analyzed by Mauss in *The Gift*. The infinite replicability of digital goods
means that there is no basis for competitive sacrifice characteristic of
potlatch: the giver gives nothing up. Giesler's claim that Napster fits
the mold of a "cybernetic gift-giving" is an instructive example. His
own extensive description shows how file sharing on Napster departs
radically from every other gift economy in anthropological literature,
thus ultimately proving, against his intentions, that the gift is not an
appropriate analytic framework for piracy and file-sharing cultures.

The Invisible Committee's prefigurative politics has been criticized
by other communization groups as running counter to the antagonism
at the heart of proletarian movement. "There is no 'outside', or 'line of
flight', but only a thinking through of this immanent contradiction and
antagonism secreted within capitalist exploitation of labor to extract
value" (Noys 10). The authorial collective Endnotes explicitly rules out
sharing communities or commons as the basis for communization:

> For us, communization does not signify some general positive
> process of "sharing" or "making common." It signifies the specific
> revolutionary undoing of the relations of property constitutive of
> the capitalist class relation. Sharing as such – if this has any mean-
> ing at all – can hardly be understood as involving this undoing
> of capitalist relations, for various kinds of "sharing" or "making
> common" can easily be shown to play important roles within capi-
> talist society without in any way impeding capitalist accumulation.
> Indeed, they are often essential to – or even constitutive in – that
> accumulation: consumption goods shared within families, risk
> shared via insurance, resources shared within firms, scientific
> knowledge shared through academic publications, standards and
> protocols shared between rival capitals because they are recog-
> nized as being in their common interest. In such cases, without
> contradiction, what is held in common is the counterpart to an ap-
> propriation. As such, a dynamic of communization would involve
> the undoing of such forms of "sharing", just as it would involve the
> undoing of private appropriation. ("What are We to Do?" 27)

Essentially, sharing lacks the antagonistic dimension required of a
movement bent on the abolition of the capitalist value-form. The radical dimension of piracy comes from its disregard of property and the
state – its movement as negation, rather than the positive effects of
"file sharing." Indeed, the term "file sharing" could be understood as
a kind of tactical move by pirates to redefine their practices as legal

and non-harmful, and thereby domesticate them.[7] A communization perspective, instead, values piracy's ability to upend and redistribute private property, to damage capitalist enterprise, and to destabilize division among the classes. Such activity has communism as its content, as explained by Théorie Communiste:

> In the course of revolutionary struggle, the abolition of the state, of exchange, of the division of labor, of all forms of property, the extension of the situation *where everything is freely available* as the unification of human activity – in a word, the abolition of classes – are "measures" that abolish capital, imposed by the very necessities of struggle against the capitalist class. The revolution is communization; it does not have communism as a project and result, but as its very content. (41, emphasis added)

There is a theoretical reason for de-emphasizing the role of consciousness in communization. Too much means the proletariat identifies as the "working class," and thus acts shores up its identity (via pay raises, self-management of work, and other initiatives) rather than abolishing itself. As communism means the abolition of classes at the hands of the proletariat, the proletariat must itself be self-abolishing. How does political action unfold without a concrete identity or organizations pushing it forward?

In its analysis of the 2011 London riots, the journal SIC provides an account. The post-Fordist restructuring of capital, and its accompanying entrepreneuralization of the working class (see Chapter 1), effectively divided the class into individuals, a triumph affirmed by neoliberal ideology. This worked to

> transform the working class from a collective subject confronting the bourgeoisie into a sum of proletarians, every one of whom is individually related to capital and each other, without the mediation of the practical experience of a common class identity and workers' organisations that would represent the class as a recognised social partner, accepted to participate at the table of collective bargaining.

However, class struggle is not simply a voluntary undertaking, but emerges continually. Because "the reproduction of the relation of exploitation is contradictory," attempts to resolve or challenge capitalism through its contradictions spontaneously surface. It is because older left organizations haven't recognized the new proletarian situation under post-Fordism that the riots were not recognized as a communist movement itself. The relevant fact of the current conjuncture for communization is "the world-wide precarisation of labour power": the contradiction between capital's need to abolish unruly labor via technology and its insatiable need for labor power has reached an extreme point where the reproduction of the proletariat itself is called into question. Struggles therefore become struggles of *reproduction* rather than production.

In seeking out the means of reproduction, these struggles often take the form of looting: "Appropriation of goods or money was a transient practical critique of the commodity form, as those proletarians offensively took what they need but are objectively banned from acquiring, and in this respect the act of looting was just as important as the loot." According to SIC, with this practice "rioters momentarily questioned the commodity form but did so only at the level of exchange because this was the scope of their revolt." This "practical critique" was often mistaken, even by critics of capitalism, as a kind of "consumer entitlement," the same charge often leveled at pirates. In fact, it reveals the terrain of struggle under precarity. It is a terrain overdetermined, on the one hand, by increased precarity and immiseration, and, on the other, by an elevated presence of guard labor.

SIC also critiques the riot itself – after all, it did not lead to communism. Why did it fail? In part, because loot was resold, thus reinserting the capitalist form of value. Struggles need to be generalized. "For looting for sale to be overcome, the existence of exchange has to be widely questioned in a generalised communising struggle." In a sense, this is what widespread piracy accomplished. Not only do people take as they need but, as a number of commentators have pointed out, increasingly disdain to pay for music at all ("Siren Song"; Wohlsen). The value-form itself is under attack.

While SIC provides no theory on how to generalize such a communist struggle, piracy provides an answer that aligns with the Invisible Committee's prioritization of "multiplication of opacity," which follows Foucault's dictum that "visibility is a trap" (*Discipline and Punish* 200). The codes and cultures of online piracy at its deepest levels insist on compulsory anonymity through proliferating darknets, digital networks which cloak themselves in increasing levels of security and secrecy. In a controversial report, Microsoft researchers concluded that file-sharing darknets are essentially impossible to eradicate entirely.

> There seem to be no technical impediments to darknet-based peer-to-peer file sharing technologies growing in convenience, aggregate bandwidth and efficiency. The legal future of darknet-technologies

is less certain, but we believe that, at least for some classes of user, and possibly for the population at large, efficient darknets will exist. (Biddle et al. 14)

From these darknets, pirates possess the ability to intervene in the flows of informational commodities over the Internet, an ability which can never be eliminated, and which draws upon the skills and practices developed by decades of digital piracy. It is a realm of freedom and autonomy from the state and, to some extent, capitalist social relations (exchange of commodities, especially illegal ones, thrives on darknets). From a communization perspective, darknets are potentially a site for the development of organized practices to contest the capitalist system via the conscious and politicized self-activity of computer users. Piracy thus emerges as an alternative arrangement of work and consumption, based around self-management, voluntaristic association, and noncommercial rewards, such as status. Status is linked to skill, the feature that preserves pirate autonomy. In a sense, organized piracy not only posits an alternative vision to the neoliberal capitalist Internet, but it actually achieves it, however, partially and temporarily. Pirates are their own invisible committee.

Of course, we may be at the end of the golden age of piracy, as anonymity is increasingly abandoned and new commercial services have arisen to reinsert commodity relations into media consumption. And of course, the proletariat cannot reproduce itself on free music and movies alone. In the final analysis, the drawbacks of communization theory – its inability to adequately theorize political activity beyond riots, its lack of interest in consolidating anti-capitalist gains, its narrow focus on insurrection at the expense of any other kind of activity – are also the drawbacks to the politics enacted by piracy.

Conclusions

In conclusion, piracy is a kind of enacted struggle over property, a roving antagonism born, not out of the conscious political motivations of pirates, but out of the contradictions of a specific political and economic context: one rooted in increasing automation, control, and militarization. While political organizations surrounding pirate concerns have emerged in places like Scandinavia, they consist of a minority of individuals engaged in piracy, and thus fail to wholly represent pirate politics. Pirate politics constitute a real movement, one that does not have precise demands, or developed organizational structures, but one which emerges in the cracks and contradictions of 21st-century digital capitalism, in the spheres of production and distribution of commodities. It cannot be easily reconciled with insurgent capitalist competition, with social democratic reformism, or with militant anti-capitalism. It is, no more and no less, an important form of social antagonism, an assemblage of techniques, technologies, and tactics that delineate one kind of real movement against the established order.

What remains to be discussed is an even wider view of piracy, one that is not circumscribed to the digital networks of the Internet, but rather brings into the discussion the forms it takes in a globalized political economy of media. This will be undertaken in the next chapter.

Notes

1 This is, in some sense, a flipped version of Michael Strangelove's study, which examines Situationist-inspired detournement as evidence of pirate anti-capitalism. Strangelove concerns himself primarily with symbols and their manipulation, rather than the exchange of digital artifacts, such as music or movie files, that stand in for consumer commodities. To find anti-capitalism in piracy, he examines anti-consumerist activism, rather than any reckoning with the production of value, and his study is of limited use to examining file sharing.
2 Marx discusses teaching and the production of surplus value in *Capital* Vol. 1, Chapter 16.
3 Kjøsen makes a similar mistake with regard to space. He notes that digital commodities are located on server farms rather than warehouses, but curiously argues that the former are evidence that digital commodities have no physical presence. Rather, they indicate the materiality and physicality of even digital information: it has spatial presence, albeit a much smaller one.
4 One of the most important aspects of Schwartz's research is his translation into English of many Piratbyran works that appeared exclusively in Swedish.
5 The label of "communization" is disputed among these groups, particularly Invisible Committee, but they share a number of theoretical and political characteristics such that the categorization fits.
6 Endnotes frame this in a materialist way: these institutions arose during a specific period of capitalism, but are no longer effective due to the post-Fordist restructuring of the working class ("Spontaneity, Mediation, Rupture"). It could also be understood to derive from communization's origins in the French ultraleft. In France, working-class organizations are much more institutionalized within the state than in the US.
7 See John 125–43 for one account of the emergence of the terminology of "file sharing" and its rhetorical uses.

Works Cited

Adler, Jerry. "Raging Bulls: How Wall Street Got Addicted to Light-Speed Trading." *Wired* 20.9 (3 Aug. 2012). Web. 13 April 2015.

Barbrook, Richard. "The High Tech Gift Economy." *First Monday* 3.2 (Dec. 1998). n. pag.

Bey, Hakim. *T.A.Z.: The Temporary Autonomous Zone.* Brooklyn, NY: Autonomedia, 1991.

Biddle, Peter, Paul England, Marcus Peinado, and Bryan Willman. "The Darknet and the Future of Content Distribution." Microsoft Corporation, 2002. Web. 14 June 2014.

Burkart, Peter. *Pirate Politics: The New Information Policy Contests.* Cambridge, MA: MIT P, 2014.

Carpou, Zoe. "Robots, Pirates, and the Rise of the Automated Takedown Regime: Using the DMCA to Fight Piracy and Protect End-Users." *Columbia Journal of Law and Arts* 39.4 (2015–2016): 551–589.

Davis, Jim and Michael Stack. "The Digital Advantage." *Cutting Edge: Technology, Information Capitalism and Social Revolution.* Eds. Jim Davis, Thomas A. Hirschl, and Michael Stack. London: Verso, 1998. 121–144.

Durand, Rodolphe and Jean-Phillippe Vergne. *The Pirate Organization: Lessons from the Fringes of Capitalism.* Boston, MA: Harvard Business Review P, 2013.

Elliott, John E. "Marx and Schumpeter on Capitalism's Creative Destruction: A Comparative Restatement." *Quarterly Journal of Economics* 95.1 (Aug. 1980): 45–68.

Endnotes Collective. "Spontaneity, Mediation, Rupture." *Endnotes* 3 (2013): n. pag. Web. 22 Apr. 2015.

———. "What are We to Do?" *Communization and its Discontents: Contestation, Critique and Contemporary Struggles.* Ed. Benjamin Noys. Brooklyn, NY: Minor Compositions, 2011. 23–40.

Foucault, Michel. *Discipline and Punish: The Birth of the Prison.* Trans. Alan Sheridan. New York, NY: Vintage Books, 1977.

Giesler, Markus. "Cybernetic Gift Giving and Social Drama: A Netnography of the Napster File-Sharing Community." *Cybersounds: Essays on Virtual Music Culture.* Ed. Michael D. Ayers. New York, NY: Peter Lang International Academic Publishers, 2006. 21–55.

Hall, Gary. "Pirate Radical Philosophy." *Radical Philosophy* 173 (May–June 2012): 33–40.

Heller-Roazen, Daniel. *The Enemy of All: Piracy and the Law of Nations.* Brooklyn, NY: Zone Books, 2009.

The Invisible Committee. *The Coming Insurrection.* Los Angeles, CA: Semiotext(e), 2008.

Jayadev, Arjun and Bowles, Samuel. "Guard labor." *Journal of Development Economics* 79 (2006): 328–348.

Jessop, Bob. "Marxist Approaches to State Power." *The Wiley-Blackwell Companion to Political Sociology.* Eds. Edwin Amenta, Kate Nash, and Alan Scott. Oxford: Blackwell, 2012, 3–14.

John, Nicholas A. *The Age of Sharing.* Cambridge: Polity P, 2017.

Johns, Adrian. *Piracy: The Intellectual Property Wars from Gutenberg to Gates.* Chicago, IL: U of Chicago P, 2011.

Kjøsen, Atle Mikkola. "An Accident of Value: A Marxist-Virillian Analysis of Digital Piracy." Master's thesis, the University of Western Ontario, 2010.

Leeson, Peter. *The Invisible Hook: The Hidden Economics of Pirates*. Princeton, NJ: Princeton UP, 2011.

Marx, Karl. *Capital: A Critique of Political Economy, Volume 1*. Trans. Ben Fowkes. London: Penguin Books, 1992.

———. *Capital: A Critique of Political Economy, Volume 2*. Trans. David Fernbach. London: Penguin Books, 1993.

———. "The German Ideology." *Selected Writings*. 2nd ed. Ed. David McLellan. Oxford: Oxford UP, 2006. 175–208.

———. *Grundrisse: Foundations of the Critique of Political Economy*. Trans. Martin Nicolaus. London: Penguin Books, 1993.

Mason, Matt. *The Pirate's Dilemma: How Youth Culture Is Reinventing Capitalism*. New York, NY: Free P, 2008.

Noys, Benjamin. "The Fabric of Struggles." Communization and its Discontents: Contestation, Critique, and Contemporary Struggles. Ed. Benjamin Noys. Brooklyn: Minor Compositions, 2011. 7–17.

Mauss, Marcel. *The Gift: The Form and Reason for Exchange in Archaic Societies*. Trans. W.D. Halls. New York, NY: W.W. Norton, 1990.

Perelman, Michael. "The Rise of Guard Labor." *Dollars and Sense*. Jan.–Feb. 2010.

Rose, Frank. "Music Industry Proposes a Piracy Surcharge on ISPs." *Wired*. 13 Mar. 2008. Web. 16 June 2014.

Schumpeter, Joseph. *Capitalism, Socialism and Democracy*. New York, NY: Harper, 1975.

Schwartz, Jonas Andersson. *Online File Sharing: Innovations in Media Consumption*. London: Routledge, 2013.

SIC. "The Feral Underclass Hits the Streets: On the English Riots and Other Ordeals." *SIC: International Journal for Communization* 2 (2013): 95–128.

"Siren Song." *The Economist*. 12 May 2011.

Strangelove, Michael. *Empire of Mind: Digital Piracy and the Anti-Capitalist Movement*. Toronto: U of Toronto P, 2005.

Théorie Communiste. "Communization in the Present Tense." *Communization and Its Discontents: Contestation, Critique and Contemporary Struggles*. Ed. Benjamin Noys. Brooklyn, NY: Minor Compositions, 2011. 41–60.

Wohlsen, Marcus. "Apple and Amazon Have a Problem: People Don't Want to Buy Stuff Anymore." *Wired*. 27 Oct. 2014.

5　Global Piracy

Media piracy is, of course, not an exclusively online phenomenon. Before online file sharing emerged as a problem for the digital economy, media piracy was a problem embedded in the industrial manufacture of recordings. In fact, many pirated goods came from the exact same plants where "legitimate" copies were pressed. Owners of disc-printing factories and warehouses, often facing falling profits themselves, often produced more than the allotted number of licensed goods, and subsequently sold them through informal networks at lower prices. In the periphery, entire pirate factories sprang up, producing unauthorized goods beyond the reach of law enforcement in the Global North. According to lawyer and copyright expert William Patry, even the major labels themselves engaged in this kind of piracy: "For many years, at record labels' requests, CD plants ran what was called the 'third shift': the production of large numbers of CDs that were off the books for artists. Not existing on the books, no royalties were ever paid for the sale of these CDs" (32).

Since the rise of online file sharing, scholars and copyright reformers have been at pains to draw firm lines between digital traffic in media goods from the presence of infringing material in informal markets around the globe, especially in postcolonial urban spaces (see Chapter 1). In this chapter, I seek to push against this tendency. Rather than draw distinctions between the practices of privileged Internet users and those of pirated disc traffickers in underdeveloped economies, I seek to contextualize both as part of a larger transformations in global capitalism, specifically surrounding the labor of media and cultural production. To do this, I will begin by describing the relationship of the global margins to the core in contemporary capitalism: in other words, I will offer a brief sketch of postcolonial political economy, focusing on the capital-labor relationship, often described in terms of precarity or informality.

I will then move to examining the political economy of postcolonial piracy specifically. Piracy emerged as a component of factory production, but has since deformalized into cottage industries and local networks. These are illicit entrepreneurial operations, albeit generally considered benign and operating with tacit or explicit permission from state authorities. Much of this portion will draw from recent ethnographic work on piracy in the developing world. Finally, I will examine cultural production emerging from pirate media economies. Here I am interested not only in the cultural objects themselves, but how these objects circulate, and how new practices and new politics potentially rise from the development of informal media distribution.

Postcolonial Capitalism

Capitalism is a world system, but it does not operate by the same logic in every place all at once. For over a century, critics of global capitalism have noted the important role nonindustrialized peripheries play for developed industrial capitalism in Europe and North America, who frequently intervene politically and militarily in these regions. Lenin, linking this dominance to the dictates of capitalism, defined imperialism as "the struggle for the sources of raw materials, for the export of capital, for spheres of influence" driven by the finance capital of specific nations (270). Lenin was primarily concerned about the effects of imperialism on the imperial countries and their working classes. He had less to say about the effects on the economies of the colonized.

Later theoretical work extended Lenin's analysis to discuss the transformations in relations between core countries and former colonies after the collapse of European colonial empires. In one representative example, Kwame Nkrumah sought to outline how, in spite of successful decolonization movements in the Global South, Northern nations still exerted considerable economic and political influence. This amounted to a critique of the notion of economic "development": "foreign capital is used for the exploitation rather than for the development of the less developed parts of the world. Investment under neo-colonialism increases rather than decreases the gap between the rich and the poor countries of the world" (x). The structure of the colonial economy, which was responsible for providing markets and raw materials to the core, lingered, along with coercive military and financial relationships. In this way, old colonial powers continued to dominate postcolonial nations.

Neocolonial theory is an explicit rebuke to developmentalist narratives that posit a standard progression of economic stages by formerly colonized nations from nonindustrialized to a full free market. Instead of developing every region open to it in the same way, global capitalism proceeds unevenly, maintaining large portions of the globe without the industrial capacity of the most developed regions. But does this lack of development imply that capitalist social relations do not exist in these regions?

For dependency theorists, such as Andre Gunder Frank and Immanuel Wallerstein, Global South economies, called "underdeveloped," are, in fact, marked by capitalist social relations. As Frank puts it,

> the economic, political, social, and cultural institutions we now observe [in the underdeveloped world] are the products of the historical development of the capitalist system no less than are the seemingly more modern or capitalist features of the national metropoles of these underdeveloped countries. (5)

In these systems, underdevelopment occurs because the metropole continues to extract surplus from its former colonies, while determining institutions and policies in these nations. The structural adjustment programs and intellectual property treaties such as Trade-Related Aspects of Intellectual Property Rights (TRIPS) discussed in Chapter 1 are obvious examples. Development in wealthy nations is part and parcel of underdevelopment in poorer ones. When poorer nations are tied to the capitalist world system via trade and investment – for Frank, the "persistence of commercial rather than industrial capitalism" (17) – their continued underdevelopment is assured. This is what Nkrumah refers to as "the last stage of imperialism."

As economist Kalyan Sanyal puts it, imperialist penetration of Global South economies

> radically transforms only those sectors that either provide raw material and means of production for the industrial capitalist mode without being a source of effective competition to imports, or produce luxury commodities for the local comprador classes, which are the main allies of the imperialist power. In other sectors, such as the artisan industry, which is a potential competitor of imports, the techniques of production and division of labor are largely left unchanged despite their formal subsumption by capitalism. (19)

Sanyal modifies dependency theory with the Althusserian language of articulation: "the third world is envisaged as an articulation of capitalist and pre-capitalist modes of production, which reproduces itself over time without the former superseding the latter" (15). Pre-capitalist sectors "ensure the conditions of existence of capital by acting as sources of cheap labor and raw materials" by cheapening the value of labor-power through the existence of a large pool of subsistence laborers from which to draw (20).

However, Sanyal is critical of the functionalism and economism in the preceding accounts. There are contestatory political and ideological/cultural factors impinging on postcolonial production, not merely the needs of capitalists. The articulation of capitalist and pre-capitalist (or to put it non-teleologically, noncapitalist) production is, for Sanyal's neo-Gramscian position, a result of a politically weak bourgeoisie allying "with the old dominant classes to get into macro power on the level of the state" (31). This means, as Dipesh Chakrabarty puts it, "cultural forms of authority impact organization of production" (225). Of course, this is not specific to the postcolonial world: even Marx himself recognized, with characteristic sarcasm, that cultural matters, not only economic ones, influenced capitalist production:

> In Europe, even in England, capitalist production is still affected and distorted by hangovers from feudalism. The fact that baking, shoemaking, etc. are only just being put on a capitalist basis in England is entirely due to the circumstance that English capital cherished feudal preconceptions of "respectability." It was "respectable" to sell Negroes into slavery, but it was not respectable to make sausages, boots or bread. (*Capital* 1014 fn23)

Sanyal also argues that capitalism reproduces noncapitalist sectors due to primitive accumulation at the global level, via the structural adjustment programs administered by the World Bank and the International Monetary Fund. In other words, there is not one standard trajectory of development from feudal peasantry to class of waged proletarian workers, but a complex articulation of capitalist and noncapitalist social relations – which is to say, capitalist and noncapitalist forms of exploitation. This primitive accumulation also calls into question the narratives of capitalist development, with their affirmation that free market economies will lead, in the long term, to higher living standards and greater democracy.

One rubric under which this complex articulation has been analyzed is "informality." In Chapter 1, I discussed the parallels between the informal economy and the neoliberal ideological emphasis on entrepreneurialism and deregulation. In the post-Fordist literature, which tends to examine trends in advanced economies, informality is characterized as "flexibility," and emerges as a kind of proletarianization and immiseration of what were once stable and better remunerated forms of wage labor. In the Global South, where such forms of wage labor were rare or nonexistent, informality describes capitalist development itself. The number of workers reliant on the informal economy globally is as high as 70%; in some nations it may be as high as 90% (International Labour Office 13).

In this sense, "development" may give this process too much credit. As Mike Davis notes, average incomes fell while poverty and inequality soared in nations affected by structural adjustment: such "development" made many nations poorer than they had been before (152–8). Escalating misery in the countryside (exacerbated by land enclosures and deregulation of agricultural crops) provoked an exodus of rural inhabitants, who moved to cities in search of waged work. With weak states too poor and inefficient to establish infrastructure for new inhabitants, urbanization itself has been an informal process, characterized by slums.

As Jan Breman describes it, informality is a deliberate strategy on the part of employers to reduce labor costs. "To call the informal sector unorganized is to overlook how employers operating in this vast terrain manage to lay down the term of the contract by engaging in collective action" (20). The informal sector is part of a vast reserve army of labor that causes wage rates to decline across the board. Breman argues that while workers in the informal market appear to be entrepreneurial, often engaging in practices such as street vending or informal transportation, wage labor rather than small business ownership is actually central to informal employment practices, even though it is obscured.

Breman also describes the features of informal production.

> The most obvious characteristics of these small-scale urban industries are first, a lack of complexity in the production process, limited capital, and little use of advanced technology and second, there is less division of labour than in the formal sector. Low capital intensity restricts expansion. Enterprises are fairly small, employing no more than a dozen or so workers, usually managed by a single owner. Wages are low, based not on total hours worked but on the quantity produced. Piecework rather than time rate is the measure for the sum that workers receive weekly from their employers. The workplace is a small shop or a shed. Although workers are employed on a continuous basis, they derive no rights from the arrangement at any given moment. (177)

Informality is not merely a condition of the laborer, but also colors the process of production itself. In the next section, I describe pirate production in poor nations in the interest of illustrating how piracy is one aspect of informal labor in underdeveloped economies.

Piracy and Informality

Just as a lack of development has not meant a lack of wage relations, or even a lack of manufacturing jobs (just a lack of stable, well-paid ones), the lack of development has not prevented media consumption among the world's poor. Just as the poor must devise survival strategies and rely on traditional means to secure their existence, they too manage to procure media, including recorded music, film, and even games and software. Media consumption occurs as so much other consumption does: via informal markets and itinerant street vendors. This is the world of media piracy for the majority of the world. As Gantz and Rochester put it,

> there are those who make a living at [piracy] – with some now living in jail. They fuel a huge black market around the world, with their activities running the gamut from operating duplication factories in places like Paraguay and Thailand to "cracking" the latest software programs and distributing them free over obscure sites on the Internet to copying CDs on home computers, forging CD covers using laser printers and selling the fakes in the subways of Boston, Moscow, London, and Bangkok. (25)

Such breathless descriptions, informed by culture industry propaganda, are designed to put piracy on the agenda of law enforcement. However, the Social Science Research Council's extremely detailed report on piracy in emerging markets, by situating piracy in its economic context, presents a very different picture. Describing piracy as "a global pricing problem," the report points out that, in many parts of the world, without piracy there is no access to media: "Piracy imposes an array of costs on producers and distributors – both domestic and international – but it also provides the main form of access in developing countries to a wide range of media goods, from recorded music, to film, to software" (i). While access to media, both legal and illegal, has flourished in wealthy nations, most of the world's population is priced out of legal media consumption entirely. Piracy is the only choice.

The lack of technological development and the prevalence of poverty means that high-speed Internet access has yet to reach much of the developing world. In these places, piracy continues to be a business of physical objects, rather than purely electronic ones. These commodities must be manufactured. Due to the high costs of fixed capital behind the production of physical media, piracy was, for most of its history, the province of a few organized syndicates. As Joe Karaganis describes it, "International distribution, in these circumstances, involved the smuggling of physical goods and consequently mirrored – and sometimes shared – the distribution infrastructure for other counterfeit and contraband products" (38). Places like Ukraine and Malaysia manufactured discs, which were then trafficked through regional smuggling routes.

However, changes in technology have altered the organization of production of pirate media. "Burners and blank discs are now commodity items, and their greater availability has led to a massive expansion of local production, the displacement of smuggling, and – in many countries – a reorganization of production around small-scale, often family-based, cottage industry" (39). The disaggregation and distribution of production technologies have rendered the smuggling routes obsolete. The proliferation of relatively low-cost CD-burning equipment has multiplied the points of production of pirate goods. Now pirate production is intensely localized and intensely competitive. This has lowered prices and narrowed profit margins to the point where organized crime, in spite of culture industry claims to the contrary, has little interest in piracy.[1]

Much of research in piracy examines distribution, which is the most visible side of piracy, occurring via street markets and ambulant vendors. While this media distribution may be informal, it is not unorganized. In some areas, such as Mexico, Brazil, and Bolivia, informal street vendors have formed associations to mediate disputes and negotiate with authorities, who generally tolerate their presence. In Mexico City, street vendor organizations are treated as a source of political patronage, granting a level of formalization to an otherwise precarious form of employment. In South Africa, stiffer enforcement has driven piracy into poorer townships where "forms of distribution are organized predominantly around neighborhood networks and house-to-house vending" (104). These informal markets are a vital means for people to reproduce their labor-power cheaply, and while they occupy a precarious position, their presence is more or less constant in less developed places.

Pirate commodities must be produced before they are distributed. Production facilities are small, and often home-based. For example, in Brazil "optical disc production is primarily domestic, small-scale, and decentralized" (255). Mexican piracy is run very much as a cottage industry: "producers work out of their own homes with a few burners, using friends or family as workers" (310). Often producers keep distributors at arm's length, so that vendors shoulder all the risk of possible law enforcement action (134).[2] Vendors often perform final assembly work on the packaging themselves.

Commercial piracy is done for profit, on razor-slim margins. As such, exploitative relationships are common. Researchers continually find youth and immigrants working in pirate operations, "signs of the disposable labor strategies that minimize liability and shelter owners from arrest" (135). This is particularly true when law enforcement and competition deformalize the industry, forcing it into flexible, mobile, and precarious forms of labor. Where family- and home-based production reigns, child labor is common. The presence of production in homes and neighborhoods lends another dimension to the social factory thesis: production now occupies the space of reproduction, and the example of piracy – both a productive process and a form of consumption – neatly typifies this collapse. Street vendors, who bear the majority of the risk from law enforcement, are often immigrants. Researchers in Russia reported rumors of use of psychiatric patients and prisoners for labor (172–3). This is one way that capitalist production, premised on the wage laborer free to contract her labor-power, is, to use Sanyal's terminology, articulated with noncapitalist production, organized in patriarchy or other systems of hierarchy and privilege, rather purely through markets. Of course, actually existing capitalism has long made opportunistic use of previously existing forms of oppression and inequality, a dynamic that is often exacerbated in postcolonial pirate contexts.

This intertwining of market and nonmarket recalls the work of Karl Polanyi. Polanyi saw that capitalism, in its rush to commodify everything, risked annihilating the basis of its generation of wealth, including its workers: "not human beings and natural resources only but also the organization of capitalistic production itself had to be sheltered from the devastating effects of a self-regulating market" (138). Polanyi identifies a "double movement" operating in the development of capitalism:

> The one was the principle of economic liberalism, aiming at the establishment of a self-regulating market, relying on the support of the trading classes, and using largely laissez-faire and free trade as its methods; the other was the principle of social protection aiming at the conservation of man and nature as well as productive

organization, relying on the varying support of those most immediately affected by the deleterious action of the market – primarily,
but not exclusively, the working and the landed classes – and
using protective legislation, restrictive associations, and other
instruments of intervention as its methods. (138–9)

Just as the culture industries rely upon protective legislation and restrictions in the form of intellectual property, subsidies, and licensing
agreements to govern media markets, pirate workers draw from nonmarket sources to maintain their operations.

However, this is unstable and often unsustainable: competition,
driven by gratuitous pirate production, is fierce. Increased access to
media comes at a cost of heightened competition and lack of regulation, tendencies which erode profits. If piracy is a crisis in the political
economy of media, it is a crisis that is also due to tendencies internal to
capitalist accumulation: the way that unfettered competition serves to
undermine the conditions of capitalist accumulation.[3] Indeed, piracy
is its own crisis: the Social Science Research Council reports that disc
pirates increasingly have to compete with "free" – the availability of
pirate commodities online. It would seem, as Polanyi pointed out, that
just as capitalism requires space free from the market in order to per-
sist, so too does media, at least media organized along capitalist lines.

Yet the problems of the pirate economy are not an exception, but
the rule in informal economies. Pirate economies share many of the
features of labor in the informal sector: low pay, high rate of exploitation, and generally low productivity. It appears as an "entrepreneurialization" of labor, with capital and risk borne by the worker, and
where workers earn based on goods produced and retailed, rather
than a waged hourly rate. That this deformalization resembles formal
subsumption of the labor process further indicates that subsumption,
as previously discussed, is not a historical period of capitalist development, but a logical category that can exist in a variety of conjunctures,
especially those in which informal labor relations prevail.

Piracy vs. Empire

The development of domestic media industries in emerging economies
is of interest because, as discussed in Chapter 1, the North, the US in
particular, works to squelch national cinemas overseas by subjecting
them to untrammeled competition from its own heavily subsidized
media products. Could media piracy be part of a developmentalist
agenda to grow media economies (and most importantly, jobs) in poor

nations? Further, does piracy's antagonistic relationship to commercial exchange of media commodities, an important element of the North's economic dominance over the South, constitute ground for shaking off neocolonial relations? To put it more bluntly, is piracy anti-imperialist?

An argument could be made that piracy is an extension of imperialist domination of global media. Pirate production is local, but it is imbricated in a globalized media climate dominated by US productions. Pirates do perform a kind of work for these companies. They open up markets for media where none existed before, part of what Ramon Lobato calls "the explosion of consumer culture among the poor" (51). This consumer culture is dominated by US goods – pirate markets are parasites not only of media commodities, but of the global marketing schemes of Hollywood. While companies may not directly profit from these expanded markets, they may accrue benefits from the wider recognition of their brands and texts. In the case of software, piracy helps to establish certain standards, such as the use of Microsoft products, in emerging business cultures. "When these emerging markets begin to grow, as most did in the last decade, piracy ensures they do so along paths shaped by the powerful network and lock-in effects associated with the market leaders" (Karaganis 52). In these cases, the use of pirated corporate software pushes out free open-source alternatives (ibid).

If we take the repeated invocations of the SSRC report and other scholars that pirate copies do not represent lost sales, then piracy is best understood as an informal means of increasing access to media for potential audiences abandoned by formal distribution. These viewers-in-waiting form a kind of surplus audience unnecessary for the reproduction and expansion of the culture industries. Pirates monetize these audiences by mimicking elements of the culture industry (such as producing and selling optical discs as commodities) and uniting them with indigenous economies and networks. It is a combined and uneven development of domestic cultural production where high technology goods meet relations of production reliant on family structure and distribution networks derived from old trade routes, neighborhood networks, and ethnic diasporas.

Yet piracy is certainly a target of trade agreements widely condemned as perpetuating Northern economic hegemony, such as the TRIPS treaty. Such agreements not only require developing nations to conform to wealthy nations' intellectual property standards – an unfair proposition, since wealthy nations hold far more intellectual property. They also establish frameworks of enforcement, with a number of examples where local law enforcement and military have cooperated closely with US corporations.

As to whether piracy resists Northern cultural and economic he-gemony, the answer requires a bit more detail. SSRC researchers of-ten found ambivalence with regard to pirating of local content, but few consumers – or authorities – were especially bothered by the infringement of US goods. Many consumers express a kind of anti-Americanism by refusing to pay high prices to overseas companies for media. Some even viewed their piratical practice in a political way, as denying profits to exploitative American corporations. Local author-ities often share this opinion, and permit the piracy of US products. Perhaps more important than this (since few pirate consumers repre-sent lost sales), the localism of pirate economies keeps scarce capital within a nation's borders, rather than accrued as profits to overseas companies. This, and the ability of piratical practices to generate em-ployment, is likely the reason that media piracy is tolerated, and even encouraged, in poorer nations.

Creative Pirates

In addition to economic effects, pirate economies provide infrastruc-ture for cultural productions outside Northern hegemony. Pirate pro-ducers are not merely imitators and copyists, or engaged in simple manufacture. They also add creative and cultural labor to preexist-ing works. In addition to curating collections and fashioning cover art, subtitling and dubbing into native languages is an important contribution made by pirates in the context of a global film culture dominated by English-language fare hailing from the US. Just as piracy provides the only means of access to media for many people, unofficial subtitling provides the only translation for some languages. "With the exception of some soap operas and anime, almost no for-eign media is dubbed" in Greece (Petridis). In Russia, a subgenre of "funny translations" provides an alternate, satirical dubbing track (194–5). Pirates do a kind of necessary work of indigenizing media products for local markets. This is only possible because of the saturation of the means of media reproduction, creating locally organized economies.

As an intensely local organization of production, piracy also has be-come the basis for localized cultural production. "South African hip-hop was built on home production and pirated software," according to Natasha Primo and Libby Lloyd ("Media Piracy" 122), a phenom-enon that Adam Haupt likens to opposition to cultural imperialism. Laurent Fintoni documents that widespread piracy of the music pro-duction software Fruity Loops was instrumental to a generation of producers in local hip hop scenes in the US and the UK (Red Bull Music Academy). Tecnobrega, a regional musical style in Brazil, uses pirate networks to distribute mixes (which often contain unlicensed remixes of pop songs) as a method to promote live shows and parties (Krauskopf). In Bolivia, according to a diplomatic cable leaked by Wikileaks, a film director and at least one pop star made distribution deals with the union of pirate producers and vendors, much to the chagrin of US authorities.

Perhaps the most stunning success of piracy as a method of media distribution is the Nigerian film industry, often referred to as "Nollywood." Nollywood films are produced cheaply and in large volume; the United Nations reports that Nollywood surpasses Hollywood in the number of films produced. Contained within Nollywood are a number of distinct media ecologies, primarily organized around linguistic categories. As Lobato describes it, "Nollywood's distribution sector is controlled by an array of small-time entrepreneurs, pirates and marketers which has yet to congeal into major studios and corporations as per the Euro-American model" (56). This distribution mechanism emerged from pirate networks specializing in Hollywood and Bollywood films, as well as the authorized duplication of religious cassettes. Piracy and legitimate reproduction are inseparable. This leads to what Lobato calls "revenue leakage" as distributors, though "enough money makes its way back to producers via marketers to sustain production" (58).

Nollywood is a big business, the second largest sector of the Nigerian economy after agriculture (Economist). According to Chukwuma Okoye, "the video film provides a counter narrative to not only the silencing of the ordinary people but a remapping of the postcolonial social, cultural, and economic landscape by providing both entertainment and employment" (quoted in Lobato, 59). This remapping travels along the vast Nigerian diaspora, influencing cultural production. Several other nascent local film scenes have cropped up in sub-Saharan Africa following the Nollywood model, an example of what Alessandro Jedlowski calls "pirate transnationalism" (31). Lobato notes that with increased clout has come pressures for the industry to formalize, which would require "strong and more effective regulatory institutions" encompassing a host of issues including copyright enforcement (60). Jedlowski reports formalization initiatives centered around the Nigerian diaspora in London. These efforts tend to replicate earlier models of foreign cinema displayed in Northern metropoles: large budgets, avant-garde style, and distribution in cinemas and through streaming sites, rather than on discs.

While prevalent and highly visible in poor nations, piracy is by no means exclusive to them. Practically every major city has some level of street piracy activity, often connected to other zones of deformalized commerce, such as flea markets and trade shows, and to ethnic diasporas, which often rely on piracy to distribute niche media unavailable in certain contexts. Piracy is therefore a persistent feature of late capitalist urban space. Global capitalism's uneven development is spatially complex: zones of exclusion exist within areas of extreme wealth and development.

Piracy is also connected to alternative spheres for information. The SSRC report finds that in South Africa, for example, apartheid resistance drew on illegal distribution, as well as informal labor regimes that subverted white ownership. These laid the groundwork for contemporary pirate networks (131). The prevalence of piracy in the former Soviet Union and Warsaw Pact nations likely owes something to the history of samizdat as well. In Greece, media was tightly controlled by the state, a legacy of its dictatorship. After the financial crisis of 2008, state-run media faced enormous cuts. According to Petridis, P2P communities, carrying on the samizdat tradition, stepped into the void.

> P2P networks have played a part in the growth of an alternative public sphere because they are – in an important sense – not new. Rather, they are the current platforms for social and sharing networks that date back at least a decade.... The "big bang" of Greek P2P use took place in the middle of the decade with the establishment of the first Greek BitTorrent trackers – just in time for the larger meltdown of trust in state institutions.

These communities were quickly politicized, as crackdowns on pirate sites were immediately likened to other repressive measures taken by the Greek government during the implementation of austerity.

Sarah Harris's ethnography of cybercafes in Turkey is a fascinating account of the power of piracy when embedded in other forms of organization. Subject to crackdowns from the culturally conservative Justice and Development Party (AKP) over hysterias about indecent content and undermined by the expansion of home Internet to Turkey's middle class, cybercafes were forced into cost-cutting measures, including using unlicensed software and maintaining outdated equipment.

> By regularly failing or refusing to purchase software licenses and implement filtering and surveillance measures that drain budgets and bandwidth, operators impede government and corporate interests. At the same time, the operators coordinate, repair, and

teach in order to fill an infrastructural void for have-less users.... the generativity emerging from operators' circumventions are a prerequisite for working-class network society. (213)

In a world marked by increasing class stratification along with an entrenchment of repressive measures designed to enforce market relations, the existence of working-class networked societies or subaltern media ecologies will, by necessity, be piratical, informal, ad hoc, and parasitic on the global cultural economy, not independent of it.

Notes

1 One major exception is Russia, where state collusion protects pirate media from ruinous competition. Pirate media remains relatively expensive in Russia compared to other nations due to its protectionist climate, though researchers found no evidence of involvement with organized crime (153).
2 Again, Russia seems to be the exception, where legitimate optical disc plants run extra shifts or production lines beyond their legal quotas, in ways similar to pre-Internet piracy (170).
3 Wolfgang Streeck makes just this argument in a recent article, "How Will Capitalism End?": "having no opposition may actually be more of a liability for capitalism than an asset" (50).

Works Cited

Breman, Jan. *Footloose Labour: Working in India's Informal Economy.* Cambridge: Cambridge UP, 1996.

Chakrabarty, Dipesh. "Conditions for Knowledge of Working-Class Conditions." *Selected Subaltern Studies.* Eds. Ranajit Guha and Gayatri Chakravorty Spivak. Oxford: Oxford UP, 1988. 179–230.

Davis, Mike. *Planet of Slums.* London: Verso, 2007.

Fintoni, Laurent. "How Fruity Loops Changed Music-Making Forever." *Red Bull Music Academy Daily.* Red Bull Music Academy, 13 May 2015. Web. 12 Dec. 2015.

Frank, Andre Gunder. "The Development of Underdevelopment." *Monthly Review* 18.4 (Sept. 1966): 17–31.

Gantz, John and Jack B. Rochester. *Pirates of the Digital Millennium.* Upper Saddle River, NJ: Financial Times Prentice Hall, 2005.

Harris, Sarah. "Service Providers as Digital Media Infrastructure: Turkey's Cybercafe Operators." *Signal Traffic: Critical Studies of Media Infrastructures.* Eds. Lisa Parks and Nicole Starosielski. Urbana: U of Illinois P, 2015. 205–224.

Haupt, Adam. *Stealing Empire: P2P, Intellectual Property and Hip-Hop Subversion.* Cape Town: HSRC P, 2008.

International Labour Office. Women and Men in the Informal Economy: A Statistical Picture. 3rd ed. Geneva: International Labour Organization, 2018.

Jedlowski, Alessandro. "From Nollywood to Nollyworld: Processes of Transnationalization in the Nigerian Video Film Industry." *Global Nollywood: The Transnational Dimensions of an African Video Film Industry.* Eds. Matthias Krings and Onookome Okome. Bloomington: Indiana UP, 2013. 25–45.

Krauskopf, Ana Domb. "Tacky and Proud: Exploring Tecnobrega's Value Network." Convergence Culture Consortium White Paper, 2009.

Lenin, Vladimir Illich. "Imperialism: The Highest Stage of Capitalism." *The Lenin Anthology.* Ed. Robert C. Tucker. New York, NY: W.W. Norton, 1975. 204–274.

Lobato, Ramon. *Shadow Economies of Cinema: Mapping Informal Film Distribution.* London: British Film Institute, 2012.

Marx, Karl. *Capital: A Critique of Political Economy, Volume 1.* Trans. Ben Fowkes. London: Penguin Books, 1992.

"Media Piracy in Emerging Economies." Ed. Joe Karaganis. Social Science Research Council, 2011.

Nkrumah, Kwame. *Neo-Colonialism, the Last Stage of Imperialism.* New York, NY: International Publishers, 1966.

"Nollywood Dreams." *The Economist.* 27 July 2006. Web. 22 Apr. 2015.

Patry, William. *How to Fix Copyright.* Oxford: Oxford UP, 2011.

Petridis, Petros. "File Sharing and the Greek Crisis." *Infojustice.* 18 June 2012. Web. 23 Apr. 2015.

Polanyi, Karl. *The Great Transformation: The Political and Economic Origins of Our Time.* Boston, MA: Beacon P, 1957.

Sanyal, Kalyan. *Rethinking Capitalist Development: Primitive Accumulation, Governmentality and Post-Colonial Capitalism.* London: Routledge, 2013.

Streeck, Wolfgang. "How Will Capitalism End?" *New Left Review* 87 (May–June 2014): 35–64.

Wallerstein, Immanuel. *World-Systems Analysis: An Introduction.* Durham, NC: Duke UP, 2004.

Conclusions
The End of P2P

In an interview with Vice Magazine shortly after his release from prison, Peter Sunde, one of the founders of The Pirate Bay, expresses pessimism about Internet politics. "I have given up the idea that we can win this fight for the internet," he states, referring to battles for privacy, user autonomy, and independence from corporate control. "I think it's really important people understand this. We lost this fight" (Mollen).

In giving up on fighting for the Internet, Sunde argues that politics should refocus on "the real world" of "extreme capitalism": "stop treating internet like it's a different thing and start focusing on what you actually want your society to look like. We have to fix society, before we can fix the internet." It is a complete about-face from the articulation of pirate politics that emerged from a few years before (see Chapter 4) premised on preserving civil liberties, and even reforming the cultural economy, by defending the Internet from state interference and challenging intellectual property regulations. Instead, Sunde, an avowed socialist, strikes an accelerationist note, hoping that a right-wing president like Sarah Palin or Donald Trump can provoke a crisis in capitalism. "That would be great, because then you can finally see capitalism crashing so hard."

Sunde's abandonment of exclusively Internet-based politics for causes more resembling traditional leftist political concerns, such as employment and corporate power, is a striking about-face against the "Californian Ideology" described by Richard Barbrook and Andy Cameron: the belief that information technology alone will "empower the individual, enhance personal freedom, and radically reduce the power of the nation state." It is also, more specifically, an acknowledgement that the era of mass piracy is, if not over, ending. A combination of technological restructuring of media distribution, ideological indoctrination, and concerted legal efforts and massive deskilling of computer use has largely outflanked piracy. It is now time to ask why the pirate project, as incoherent and yet concentrated as it was, has failed.

In their critique, Barbrook and Cameron remark upon the resemblance of the hacker vanguard's politics to "Jeffersonian democracy." In Chapter 2, I discussed the similarities between the political and economic horizon of copyright reformers and those of Thomas Jefferson, whom they often cite. Jefferson's ideal productive arrangement of society was small individual landowners and petty producers: the yeoman farmer. Jefferson believed that individual self-sufficiency guaranteed a democratic society. The abundance of land in the New World and the willingness to expropriate it from the indigenous peoples living there gave his fantasy a plausibility and attraction many Americans still feel today.

However, Jefferson's yeoman farmer democracy is only one expression of the belief in a society organized on the basis of the petty producer. In 19th-century Europe, where most land had long been tied up in hereditary estates, large and small, the yeoman farmer ideal held far less influence. Without a belief in abundant land, there could be no illusion of a blank canvas on which a new society could be created: some kind of revolutionary change would have to occur within and against the old one. And so a similar, yet distinct, political philosophy sprang up in France among a similar social base of artisans and craftsmen – those who tended to control their own work process and own their own tools – who made up a significant part of the French economy. As they were used to an individualized mode of production, they too believed that self-sufficiency guaranteed liberty and prosperity. The belief that society should be organized along the lines of petty individual commodity producers, without interference from the state – a belief remarkably consonant with pirates and other digital utopians – found its most powerful expression in the ideas of Pierre-Joseph Proudhon.

An anarchist and influential member of the International Workingmen's Association of which Karl Marx was also a part, Proudhon's ideas were especially popular in his native France, where the economy was rooted far more deeply in small-scale artisanal production than the industrial-scale capitalism Marx experienced in Britain. His first major work, *What Is Property?* (Proudhon's pithy answer: property is theft), caught the attention of Marx, who admired the work's thrust and style, even while he criticized its grasp of the science of political economy. After attempting to win over Proudhon by teaching him political economy and Hegelian dialectics, Marx became a vehement critic of Proudhon's ideas, which held more sway over the First International than Marx's own.

Proudhon was critical of the capitalism of his day, but made his criticisms, along with his ideas for a better society, from the perspective of a specific class. Rather than analyze, as Marx did, the contradictions of capitalism through the figure of the proletarian, who possesses nothing but their own capacity to work, Proudhon understood capitalism from the perspective of an artisanal small producer, who owns and labors with their own small-scale means of production. In David McNally's survey of 18th- and 19th-century radical political economy, he summarizes Proudhon's beliefs. Proudhon

> envisages a society a small independent producers – peasants and artisans – who own the products of their personal labour, and then enter into a series of equal market exchanges. Such a society will, he insists, eliminate profit and property, and "pauperism, luxury, oppression, vice, crime and hunger will disappear from our midst." Here again we encounter a clarion call for the realization of justice and equality through market exchange among petty producers. (140)

Because of his petty producer standpoint, which collapses the categories of ownership of the means of production and labor, Proudhon believed exploitation occurred in exchange, rather than, as Marx argued, in the production process. Since small producers own their own tools and depend largely on their own labor, they tend to view exploitation as a result of unfair market transactions.

As McNally summarizes,

> Proudhon depicts exploitation as a product of monopoly and a violation of the true principles of commodity exchange. Under the prevailing system, he asserts, "there is irregularity and dishonesty in exchange," a problem exemplified by monopoly and its perversion of "all notions of commutative justice." The result of these market irregularities is that "the price of things is not proportionate to their value: it is larger or smaller according to an influence which justice condemns, but the existing economic chaos excuses – Usury." (142)

This particular view of economic injustice begets its own version of how best to change it. Proudhon's revolutionary vision centers on the end of monopolies and currency reform, two ways that "monopolists" intervened in the smooth functioning of the market. He railed against "middlemen, commission dealers, promoters, capitalists, etc., who, in the old order of things, stand in the way of producer and consumer," rather than wage labor and ownership of the means of production, the major political concerns of Marx and his followers (*General Idea of the Revolution in the Nineteenth Century* 90). Indeed, as McNally shows, blaming economic woes on "monopolists" and "middle-men" ran rife in popular critiques of political economy during the 17th and 18th centuries, leading many radicals to call for free trade as a solution to widespread poverty.

Proudhon's misplaced emphasis on villainous monopolies is part of a greater error in diagnosing the momentous changes in the 19th-century economy: a neglect of the centrality of massive industrial-scale production to mature capitalism. In the first volume of *Capital*, Marx argues that petty production was a historical phenomenon that would give way to capitalist production:

> Private property which is personally earned, i.e., which is based, as it were, on the fusing together of the isolated, independent working individual with the conditions of his labour, is supplanted by capitalist private property, which rests on exploitation of alien, but formally free labour. (928)

As producers compete and more and more producers fail and are proletarianized, capital – and with it, labor – concentrates. Work is socialized through its mediation by machinery. As Marx puts it in his book-length critique of Proudhon *The Poverty of Philosophy*, "In large-scale industry, Peter is not free to fix for himself the time of his labor, for Peter's labor is nothing without the co-operation of all the Peters and all the Pauls who make up the workshop."

By combining varying levels of individual productivity within the factory through machines which themselves are the product of so-cial labor, capitalism's dynamics create a historically novel form of production, along with new forms of culture and social relations. As Engels puts it in *Socialism: Utopian and Scientific*,

> The spinning wheel, the handloom, the blacksmith's hammer, were replaced by the spinning-machine, the power-loom, the steam-hammer; the individual workshop, by the factory implying the co-operation of hundreds and thousands of workmen. In like manner, production itself changed from a series of individual into a series of social acts, and the production from individual to social products. The yarn, the cloth, the metal articles that now come out of the factory were the joint product of many workers,

through whose hands they had successively to pass before they were ready. No one person could say of them: "I made that; this is my product."

The socialization of production under the development of the means of production – the necessity of greater collaboration and the reliance on past labors in the form of machines – gives way to a radical redefinition of the relationship to one's output. No one can claim a product was made by them alone; rather, production demands to be recognized as social. To put it in the language of cultural production, there can be no author. Or, in another implicit recognition that the work of today relies on the work of many others, past and present: everything is a remix.

The Politics of Socialization

What are the politics of conceptualizing the labor process as socialized? Management scholar Paul Adler, in a discussion of the politics of labor process theory, emphasizes the progressive aspect of socialization, something so neglected by studies of organization that he refers to his position as "the paleo-Marxist view." According to Adler, labor process studies have focused heavily on the autonomy of the worker, which tends toward "nostalgic regret" for the time of independent craftsmen, the same disposition held by Proudhon. "Autonomy is merely the converse of interdependence," he states, but that "interdependence can take either coercive or collaborative forms" (1319). It is ultimately alienated capitalist relations of production, in the form of private property and the class system, which make interdependence seem coercive: "instead of a broadening association of producers progressively mastering their collective future, this interdependence appears, at least at first, in the form of intensified coercion by quasi-natural laws of the market over firms and by corporate bureaucracy over workers" (1324). Acknowledging the socialization of production, as well as recognizing interdependence rather than fighting against it, is the grounds for the politics of creating a more egalitarian world.

Yet even as remix culture, sampling, and peer production point toward the socialization of cultural production mediated through digital networks, pirates, and copyright reformers consistently invoke the Proudhonian precepts described above.[1] In describing intellectual property rights as preserving "monopolies" and "gatekeepers" rather than securing ownership means of production, writers such as Lawrence Lessig and Cory Doctorow prioritize the need for small independent producers to maintain their working conditions and maximize their market chances. This is viewpoint that sees the Internet as an engine for individual empowerment against large-scale corporate control.

This empowerment stems from the purported ability of the Internet to disrupt corporate "middlemen" through technologies that work "peer-to-peer," thereby eliminating meddlesome and exploitative intermediaries. In technical terms, this disruption is referred to as "disintermediation": the removal of intermediaries, often by means of networked technologies. Geographer Mark Graham begins his elaboration of the concept by pointing to the hold it has among theorists of the Internet and development, including the sociologist Manuel Castells: "Direct economic links between producers and consumers are often argued to provide large benefits to both producers and consumers because the surpluses that were once extracted by middlemen can be redivided into the disintermediated commodity chain" (777). Graham traces the emphasis on the ill effects of middlemen to modernization theory, the belief that all nations, relieved of barriers to joining the global market, will follow identical paths of economic development. These beliefs "have led some practitioners of development to attempt to replicate the successes of Western firms such as Amazon.com... successes have thus far not been forthcoming."

Graham's proposal for solving the failure of disintermediation is the conscious creation of "cybermediaries," planned "middlemen" who assist small producers in accessing global supply chains. Such a solution, in light of the role of piracy, is both ironic and completely appropriate. It is ironic, in that the disintermediating effects of the Internet leave a vacuum requiring new and better, more technologically adept, intermediaries to fill it. And this is appropriate because pirate economies, whether for profit, for politics, or simply for mischief, have always relied on "cybermediaries": pirates were the first, and, for a time, the chief cybermediaries for digital media online. The abolition of middlemen, gatekeepers, of mediation, in general, that so captures Internet revolutionaries has never been achieved. Something always remains in the way.

What this means is that the now-ebbing buzzword of pirate disintermediation, "peer-to-peer," has always been an illusion. In digital networks, there can be no direct connection from one computer to another. Between peers stand levels of mediation – protocols, algorithms, interfaces, language – often grouped into a single software package, whether Napster or a BitTorrent client. In fact, "peer-to-peer" was Napster's ultimately unsuccessful alibi in its defense against charges that it knowingly assisted copyright infringement. Napster disclaimed any responsibility for activities of its users: what they did between themselves was a private choice that Napster had no control over. It has been used as an alibi for the other prosecuted software services ever since.

Disintermediation, at least in the cultural economy, is exaggerated, if not mythical. It relies upon the fantasies of immediacy and independence that are cornerstones of the larger ideologies of the individual "freedom" granted by computers and digital networks. Pirates did not destroy intermediaries, but merely developed technologies that would, they hoped, replace obsolete intermediaries such as record labels and industry trade organizations such as the Motion Picture Association of America (MPAA). Instead, new commercial cybermediaries, such as Netflix and Spotify, have usurped this role, and many artists experience greater exploitation and less power than before the disruption of the music industry, and are still impelled to sign unfavorable recording contracts. How could the piracy wave have shaken out like this?

Piracy as Platform

One useful way to describe the role of Napster, The Pirate Bay, and other "cybermediaries" of pirate ecosystems is as platforms. The term, as Tarleton Gillespie describes it, condenses several metaphors at once: both computational and architectural – "an infrastructure that supports the design and use of particular applications" (349), as well as political. "It implies a neutrality with regards to activity" which "suggests a progressive and egalitarian arrangement" (350). In the aftermath of Web 2.0, platforms have been likened to the architecture of civil society – "they afford an opportunity to communicate, interact or sell" (351). This has led the companies who own platforms to lobby against regulating them, often successfully: while the limited liability clause of the Digital Millennium Copyright Act has failed Napster and other pirate platforms, it has protected YouTube and its parent company Google, which profit from immense amounts of pirated content uploaded by users.

Ultimately, while platforms of all sorts pitch themselves as neutral, largely as a rhetorical move to limit liability, Gillespie argues that in their position in media ecology and their political resistance to regulation "they are more like traditional media than they care to admit" (359). As Laura DeNardis describes it, "The virtual and material infrastructures [intermediaries] manage, and the policy decisions embedded within these platforms... inherently embed public interest concerns" (726). That is to say, they are inherently political, and can be politicized. In fact, rather than abolish platforms and other intermediaries, acknowledging their necessity, and the role they play in socialization, following Adler's intervention, could be the way to develop a politics of socialized cultural and digital labor.

Peer-to-peer's failure stemmed from the fact that, in its zeal to attack and effectively replace intermediaries (even as it disavowed doing so), it misdiagnosed both the composition of creative workers and the root source of exploitation, much as Marx argued Proudhon did. It never coherently challenged the idea that the cultural economy should function along the lines of petty commodity production and the myths of artistic creation that accompany these views. A song, a film, an image, even an idea – none of these can be created *ex nihilo* from a Romantic individual genius. Reliant, as Proudhon was, on the figure of the individual petty-bourgeois artisan as the driving force behind cultural production, most commentators' solutions fall into Proudhon's failed strategies: if artists could own what they create, and reap the full profits without intermediaries such as record labels, their situation would improve.

However, while the link between creative labor and the petty-bourgeois viewpoint of production discussed previously is indeed tenacious, it no longer pertains to cultural production today. The contemporary production of culture under capitalism, sutured to a technical apparatus fashioned from dead labor and meant for producing commodities for profit, has been socialized within an immense global "factory" made up of layers of formal and informal workers operating at the points of production, distribution, and consumption: this is, in a sense, how I have attempted to theorize the Internet in this work. Inside the global factory of the capitalist Internet, the "artist" is a special designation for a relatively privileged laborer who makes only a portion of the cultural commodity. As Nicolas Brown puts it, in this conjuncture "whatever is genuinely inassimilable in artistic labor would cease to make any difference" even as artists are compelled to think of themselves as "entrepreneurs," the contemporary jargon for petty bourgeois. But laborers they are, and to mistake their position within production and accumulation is to begin one's politics on the wrong foot.

A progressive politics of digital culture would recognize the socialization of labor, and understand that politics must flow from that fact. Creative workers would align with others in the production chain as a class, and form the kinds of organizations, such as unions, that have been the vehicles of class politics, with the aim of controlling the means of production, not simply one's "own" products. In the current media ecosystem online, this might mean democratic control over platforms, the technical architecture for so much of digital cultural production. Then the apparatus of cultural production could be controlled democratically, rather than by the despotism of markets and private profit. Indeed, recent works on "platform cooperativism," emerging from discussions of digital labor, point in just this direction (Schneider, Scholz), as do initiatives within digital platform companies such as the Tech Workers Coalition, where privileged digital workers recognize and stand with workers whose labor is just as essential to the Internet (D'Onfro).

Piracy unsettled the existing arrangements of cultural production, but, severed from any comprehensive critique of the dominant ideologies of cultural production, no new politics could fill the void. Pirates created a powerful, technologically enhanced juggernaut against intellectual property, but without a critique of intellectual property *as private property*, the old relations of production remained intact. The P2P era has ended; indeed, it never truly began.

Note

1 For a more extensive treatment of this point, see Mueller, "Digital Proudhonism," *boundary 2*, July 31, 2018.

Works Cited

Adler, Paul. "The Future of Critical Management Studies: A Paleo-Marxist Critique of Labour Process Theory." *Organization Studies* 28.9 (Sept. 2007): 1313–1345.

Barbrook, Richard and Andy Cameron. "The Californian Ideology." *Science as Culture* 6.1 (1996): 44–72.

Brown, Nicholas. "The Work of Art in the Age of its Real Subsumption under Capital." *Nonsite*. 13 Mar. 2012. Web. 17 Feb. 2016.DeNardis, Laura. "Hidden Levers of Internet Control: An Infrastructure-Based Theory of Internet Governance." *Information, Communication & Society* 15.5 (June 2012): 720–738. Web. 15 Feb. 2016.

Doctorow, Cory. "Information Doesn't Want to Be Free: Laws for the Internet Age." *Scientific American*. 12 Dec. 2014. Web. 22 Feb. 2016.

D'Onfro, Jillian. "Google Walkouts Showed What the New Tech Resistance Looks Like, with Lots of Cues from Union Organizing." *CNBC*. 3 Nov. 2018. Web. 30 Dec. 2018.

Engels, Friedrich. *Socialism: Utopian and Scientific*. Trans. Edward Aveling. Marxists Internet Archive, 2003. Web. 16 Feb. 2016.

Gillespie, Tarleton. "The Politics of 'Platforms.'" *New Media and Society* 12.3 (2010): 347–364.

Marx, Karl. *Capital: A Critique of Political Economy, Volume 1*. Trans. Ben Fowkes. London: Penguin Books, 1992. Print.

————. "On Proudhon." *The International Workingmen's Association*. Marxists Internet Archive. n.d. Web. 16 Feb. 2016.

————. *The Poverty of Philosophy*. New York, NY: International Publishers, 1973. Print.

McNally, David. *Against the Market: Political Economy, Market Socialism and the Marxist Critique*. London: Verso, 1993.

Mollen, Joost. "Pirate Bay Founder: 'I Have Given Up.'" *Motherboard*. 11 Dec. 2015. Web. 20 Feb. 2016.

Mueller, Gavin. "Digital Proudhonism." *boundary 2*. 31 July 2018.

Proudhon, Pierre-Joseph. *General Idea of the Revolution in the Nineteenth Century*. Trans. John Beverly Robinson. Mineola, NY: Dover Publications, Inc., 2003.

Schneider, Nathan. "Owning is the New Sharing." *Shareable*. 21 Dec. 2014. Web. 16 Feb. 2016.

Scholz, Trebor. "Platform Cooperativism: Challenging the Sharing Economy." *Rosa Luxemburg Stiftung*. Jan. 2016. Web. 16 Feb. 2016.

Index

Note: Page numbers followed by 'n' denote endnotes.

acceleration, piracy and 82–9
Adler, Paul 118, 121
Adorno, Theodor 10
Agreement on Trade-Related Aspects of Intellectual Property Rights (TRIPS) 21
AKP *see* Justice and Development Party (AKP)
Alderman, John 65
Altair BASIC program 30
Althusserian language 41, 101
Althusser, Louis 5
Andersson, Jonas 70, 82
ANSI art 62
anti-capitalism 89, 96, 96n1
autonomist: account 10–11; critique 49; Marxism 2, 8, 45, 47; position 9

Barbrook, Richard 43–4, 91, 114, 115
BBS *see* Bulletin Board Systems (BBS)
Becker, Gary 17
Beck, Glenn 91
Benjamin, Walter 68
Benkler, Yochai 35; political economy 43
The Birth of Biopolitics (Foucault) 17
BitTorrent protocol 70, 71, 74n6, 77
Bollier, David 36
Bologna, Sergio 11
Boltanski, Luc 12
Bourdieu, Pierre 15
Bourriard, Nicolas 28

Boutang, Yann-Moulier 46
Bowles, Samuel 88–9
Boyle, James 39, 40; Second Enclosure Movement 46
Braverman, Harry 67
Brazil 105–6, 110
Breman, Jan 103
Brenner, Robert 8
Brown, Nicolas 121
Brown, Wendy 16–18
Bulletin Board Systems (BBS) 2, 59–64, 66
Burkart, Peter 73, 81–3

Caffentzis, George 8, 49
"The Californian Ideology" (Barbrook and Cameron) 43–4, 114
Cameron, Andy 43–4, 114, 115
Capital (Marx) 7, 85
capitalism 1, 18, 36, 41, 80–3, 106, 111, 116, 117, 121; cognitive 45–50; contradiction 20; core of 78; crises in 8, 9; profit rate in 7; postcolonial 100–4; restructuring 4, 12–15
Castells, Manuel 19, 119
Castoriadis, Cornelius 32, 34
de Certeau, Michel 32
Chakrabarty, Dipesh 102
Cherki, Eddy 64
Cheyette, Frederic L. 80
Chiapello, Eve 12
class composition 11
Cleaver, Harry 9–11

Code and Other Laws of Cyberspace
    (Lessig) 58
cognitive capitalism 29, 45–50
Coleman, Biella 33
Coleman, E. Gabriella 38
colonial economy, structure of 100
The Coming Insurrection 91
commercial piracy 106
commodification 13, 21, 31, 35, 57,
    63, 91
commodity capital 85
commodity production 35, 121
Communist Manifesto (Marx) 78
communization 3, 89–95, 96n5, 96n6
computer: animation and music
    73n1; hacker culture 29–32;
    networks 57; personal 4, 59; piracy
    63; programmers and hackers 28;
    underground 31–2, 48, 62
The Condition of Post-Modernity
    (Harvey) 14
Content Identification systems 72
Content Scramble System (CSS) 64
*Contribution to the Critique of
    Political Economy* (Marx) 34–5
control mechanisms 32, 58
Copernican revolution 9, 52
copy protections 32, 57, 58
copyright law 33
cracked programs 62
cracktros 62, 73n1
Creative Commons 36–44
creative destruction 38, 77–9
Crow, Sheryl 69
Cyber-Proletariat
    (Dyer-Witheford) 50

Dafermos, George 34
Dalla Costa, Maria 6
darknets 94, 95
Davis, Jim 86
Davis, Mike 103
Debord, Guy 10
deformalization 19, 107
Deleuze, Gilles 31, 58
Deleuzian-inflected theorization 81
DeNardis, Laura 120
digital capitalism 29, 90, 96
digital commodities 63, 84–7, 96n3
digital culture 1–4, 29, 37, 40, 91, 121

Digital Millennium Copyright Act
    (DMCA) 37, 64, 72, 88, 120
digital networks 31, 52, 57, 60, 61, 83,
    94, 96, 118–20
digital piracy 57–9; Bulletin Board
    Systems 59–64; massification of
    64–70; streaming 70–3
digital pirate politics 83
digital political economy 28–9; free
    culture and Creative Commons
    36–44; free software 32–6; hacker
    culture 29–32; immaterial labor
    and cognitive capitalism 45–50;
    labor-power 50–3
Digital Rights Management
    systems 71
disciplinary institutions 31
disruptive innovation 78, 80
DIY *see* Do-It-Yourself (DIY)
DMCA *see* Digital Millennium
    Copyright Act (DMCA)
Doctorow, Cory 118–19
Do-It-Yourself (DIY) 77, 79
domestic media industries,
    development of 107
Duménil, Gerard 8
Durand, Rodolphe 81
Dyer-Witheford, Nick 9, 50

economic development, notion of 100
economic liberalism, principle of 106
Ek, Daniel 72
Engels, Friedrich 117
entrepreneurialization, of labor 107

Facebook 52, 53
Fanning, Sean 66, 67, 69
file sharing 2, 64, 69, 71, 77, 78, 81–3,
    89, 92–4, 99
File Transfer Protocol (FTP) 64
Fintoni, Laurent 109
firewalls, control mechanism 32
First Amendment rights 38
flexible accumulation 15
Florida, Richard 40
Ford, Henry 6
Fordism: *vs.* post-Fordism 31;
    working classes of 28; *see also*
    post-Fordism
Fordism-Keynesianism 6–12, 18

foreign capital 100
formal subsumption 47, 48
Foucault, Michel 31, 41, 94;
    neoliberalism analysis 17
France 96n6, 115
Frank, Andre Gunder 101
Free Culture movement 2, 36–45, 50
free labor 52
Free Software movement 2, 30, 32–6,
    38, 41, 42, 48, 57, 58
French economy 115
Friedman, Milton 16
Frow, John 20
Fruity Loops 109–10
FTP *see* File Transfer Protocol
    (FTP)
Fuchs, Christian 52

Gambino, Federico 24n1
Gantz, John 67, 104
Gates, Bill 30
Gemeinschaft 82
General Public License (GPL) 33, 34
The German Ideology (Marx) 4
Giesler, Markus 92
The Gift (Mauss) 92
Gillespie, Tarleton 58, 120
Global North 21; law enforcement
    in 99
global piracy: *vs.* empire 107–9;
    and informality 104–7; pirate
    economies 109–12; postcolonial
    capitalism 100–4
Global South 3, 101;
    decolonization of 9
GNU General Public Licenses 33
Gnutella 69–70
Goldman, Eric 61
Golub, Alex 38
Google 52, 74n7, 87, 120
GPL *see* General Public License
    (GPL)
Graham, Mark 119
Grammar of the Multitude
    (Virno) 49
Gramsci, Antonio 6, 11
Grokster 74n5
Grundrisse (Marx) 10, 45, 49, 84
guard labor 88–9, 94
Guzman, Andrea 66

hacker culture 2, 29–32, 44, 59
hacking, phreaking, anarchy and
    viruses (HPAV) 60
Haight, Charles 58, 60
Hall, Gary 91
Hall, Stuart 10
Hardcore Computing 58, 59
Hardt, Michael 44, 45, 48, 49, 52
Hargadon, Michael A. 60
Harrison, Bennett 14
Harris, Sarah 111
Harvey, David 14–16, 18
Haupt, Adam 109
Hayek, Friedrich 38
Heinrich, Michael 7
Heller-Roazen, Daniel 81
Hesmondhalgh, David 21
Hill, Mako 33
homo oeconomicus 17
Howkins, John 40
HPAV *see* hacking, phreaking,
    anarchy and viruses (HPAV)

IBM *see* International Business
    Machines (IBM)
immaterial labor 29, 45, 47–50
industrial paradigm 5
inefficient distribution systems 79
informal economy 19, 20, 24n2, 102,
    103, 107
informality 19, 20, 99, 102–7
informal organization 32, 34, 43, 53, 70
information economy 13–14
innovation 5, 11, 13, 15, 20, 21, 23,
    38, 39, 44, 46, 48, 73, 78, 80
Intel 61
intellectual labor 21, 43, 49
intellectual property 2, 20–4, 29;
    restrictions 31; rights 118
International Business Machines
    (IBM) 36
International Working men's
    Association 115
Internet-based politics 114
Internet Relay Chat (IRC) 64, 66
Invisible Committee 90, 91, 92, 94,
    95, 96n5
The Invisible Committee:
    multiplication of opacity 94;
    prefigurative politics 92

The Invisible Hook (Leeson) 79
IRC *see* Internet Relay Chat (IRC)

Jayadev, Arjun 88–9
Jedlowski, Alessandro 110
Jeffersonian democracy 115
Jefferson, Thomas 39, 43, 44, 115
Jenkins, Henry 52
Jessop, Bob 6, 8, 13, 46, 47–8, 88
Joel, Billy 69
Johns, Adrian 79
Jones, Steve 66
Justice and Development Party (AKP) 111

Karaganis, Joe 105
Kelty, Chris 38, 58
Keynesian Welfare National State 6
Kjøsen, Atle 83–6, 96n3
Kleiner, Dmytri 40, 41, 68
knowledge economy 13–14

'law of value' 49
Lazzarato, Maurizio 45
Leeson, Peter 79
Lenin, Vladimir Illich 100
Lessig, Lawrence 37–8, 40, 42, 44, 58, 82, 118–19
Lévy, Dominique 8
Liberalism (Losurdo) 44
LimeWire 70
Linebaugh, Peter 39–40
Linux 34–6
Lipietz, Alain 7
living labor 7, 48, 49, 85, 86
Lloyd, Libby 109
Lobato, Ramon 71, 72, 108, 110
Losurdo, Domenico 44

Macaulay, Thomas Babington 39
McCourt, Tom 66, 73
McLeod, Kembrew 44
McNally, David 116, 117
McRobbie, Angela 23
Mandel, Ernest 7, 8
Marxist theory 1, 5, 8, 50, 83, 89
Marx, Karl 1, 7, 10, 13, 45, 47, 49, 51, 78, 84, 96n2, 102, 115–17; *Capital* 85
Marx, Nick 71

Mason, Matt 77–9
Massachusetts Institute of Technology (MIT) 33
mechanization 6, 8
Megaupload 71, 74n7
Merriden, Trevor 66
Mexican piracy 106
Meyer, Gordon 63
Microsoft 30, 34, 61, 94, 108
Mirowski, Philip 16, 21
MIT *see* Massachusetts Institute of Technology (MIT)
modernization theory 119
Mont Pélerin Society 15, 17
Moseley, Fred 7
MP3 64–71, 83
Murray, Patrick 47
"Music as a Service" 72

Napster 66–9, 74n4, 92, 119–20
National Information Infrastructure 37
Neff, Gina 22, 23
Negri, Antonio 11, 45, 48, 49, 52
neoclassical methodological framework 80
neocolonial theory 100–1
neoliberalism 2, 15–18; definition of 4; intellectual property 20, 21, 23; *vs.* post-Fordism 5
Netflix 73, 120
Neuwirth, Robert 20
New International Division of Cultural Labor (NICL) 22
NFO file 62, 63
NICL *see* New International Division of Cultural Labor (NICL)
No Electronic Theft (NET) Act (1997) 64
Nollywood model 110
nonmarket-based products 36
Noys, Ben 90, 91

Okoye, Chukwuma 110
online file sharing 99
open-source software 35
operaismo 8
O'Reilly, Tim 36, 51, 52
The Other Path (de Soto) 20
outdated business models 79

Palin, Sarah 114
Parker, Sean 66
Pashukanis, Evgeny 41, 42
passcodes, control mechanism 32
Patry, William 99
Peck, Jamie 14
peer-to-peer (P2P) networks 61, 64–71, 73, 111, 121, 122
Perelman, Michael 89
Perens, Bruce 36
personal computer (PC) 2, 4, 30, 31, 34, 57–9, 66
Philip, Kavita 42–3
piracy 1–3, 60, 100, 111; anti-capitalism in 96n1; *vs.* empire 107–9; and informality 104–7; MP3, P2P, and the massification 64–70; as platform 120–2; success of 110
piracy theorization 3; and acceleration 82–8; and communization 89–95; guard labor 88–9; as reform 81–2; Schumpeter, Joseph 77–80
Piratbyran 89–90, 96n4
Pirate Bay 70, 114
pirate commodities 60, 62, 71, 105, 107
pirate economies 107, 109–12, 119
Pirate Magazine 62
pirate organizations 61–4, 81–2
pirate politics 3, 83, 95, 114
Pirate's Dilemma (Mason) 77
pirate transnationalism 110
piratical practices 57
platform cooperativism 122
Polanyi, Karl 106, 107
political economy, of postcolonial piracy 100; *see also* digital political economy
Portes, Alejandro 19
postcolonial capitalism 100–4
postcolonial political economy 99, 100
post-Fordism 2, 4, 31; capitalism 48, 83; economy 23; Fordism-Keynesianism 6–12; intellectual property 20–2; management philosophy 12; neoliberalism *vs.* 5; production 15; worker 45
post-Fordist-neoliberal society 20

potent artistic techniques 37
The Poverty of Philosophy (Marx) 117
The Power of Women and the Subversion of the Community (Dalla Costa) 6
P2P networks *see* peer-to-peer (P2P) networks
pre-capitalist sectors 102
Primo, Natasha 109
private property 117
productive consumption 9–10
Proudhon, Pierre-Joseph 115–18, 121
Public Domain: Enclosing the Commons of the Mind (Boyle) 39
Punk Capitalism 77

RapidShare 71
Raymond, Eric 36
real subsumption 47
Recording Artists Coalition 69
Rediker, Marcus 39–40, 70
Regulation Theory 4–5
Reynolds, Laurence 46
RIAA 65, 69, 70
Rochester, Jack B. 67, 104
Ross, Andrew 23–4
Russia, funny translations in 109

Sanyal, Kalyan 101, 102, 106
Sassen, Saskia 19
The Scene 61, 64, 68
Schumpeterian imperatives 21
Schumpeter, Joseph 13; theorizing of piracy 77–80
Schwartz, Jonas Andersson 82, 83, 96n4
Second Enclosure Movement 46
The Secret Life of Walter Mitty 61
self-valorization 48
service sector employment 15
Shirky, Clay 51, 52
SIC 93, 94
Smith, Adam 16, 39
Smith, Tony 13, 43
Smythe, Dallas 51
social factory thesis 19
Socialism: Utopian and Scientific (Engels) 117
socialist and communist movement theory 9

socialization, politics of 118–20
Social Science Research Council
   (SSRC) 104, 107, 109, 111
Söderberg, Johan 34, 59
de Soto, Hernando 20
South Africa, stiffer enforcement in 105
Soviet Union 111
SPP *see* Swedish Pirate Party (SPP)
SSRC *see* Social Science Research
   Council (SSRC)
Stack, Michael 86
stagflation 7
Stallman, Richard 30, 33; developed
   alternative licenses 38; Free
   Software Foundation 37
The Stealth of Nations (Neuwirth) 20
Sterne, Jonathan 65
Storper, Michael 22
Strangelove, Michael 96n1
Streeck, Wolfgang 112n3
Subaltern Studies group 18
subsumption 46–9, 101, 107
Sunde, Peter 70, 114
Swedish Pirate Party (SPP) 81, 82
System D 20
system operators (sysops), of Bulletin
   Board Systems 60
Szerszynski, Bronislaw 46

Taylor, Frederick Winslow: scientific
   management of 32
Tech Workers Coalition 122
The Telekommunist Manifesto
   (Kleiner) 68
Temporary Autonomous Zones 91
Terranova, Tiziana 52
Théorie Communiste 93
Theories of Surplus Value (Marx) 20
Thomas, Douglas 30–1, 59

Thomas, Jim 63
Thompson, E. P. 39–40
Tickell, Adam 14
Toffler, Alvin 52
Tomaney, John 14
Torvalds, Linus 34
Toscano, Albert 12
TRIPS *see* Agreement on Trade-
   Related Aspects of Intellectual
   Property Rights (TRIPS)
Tronti, Mario 8, 9, 12
Trump, Donald 114
Turing, Alan 49

US Patent Office 33

Vercellone, Carlo 46–9
Vergne, Jean-Phillippe 81
Vice Magazine 114
Virilio, Paul 84
Virno, Paolo 48

Wacquant, Loïc 17, 18
Wallerstein, Immanuel 18
warez 59–64
Warsaw Pact 111
Wealth of Networks (Benkler) 35
Wieviorka, Michel 64
Williams, Raymond 68
Wissinger, Elizabeth 22, 23
Woodmansee, Martha 41
working class, informal economies
   and entrepreneurial restructuring
   of 18–20

YouTube 71–2, 74n7, 120

Zerowork journal 10
Zukin, Sharon 22, 23

Printed in the United States
by Baker & Taylor Publisher Services